HOSPITALITY SUPERVISION

AF663614

Vikram Jain

NAMAN PUBLISHER & DISTRIBUTORS
NEW DELHI

Published by
Sangeeta Jain for Naman Publisher & Distributors
7360-B, Prem Nagar,
Gali No.1, Shakti Nagar,
Delhi-110007
PH: 23823642, MOB.: 09013478302
E-mail: rajivjain72@ymail.com

[The responsibility for the facts stated, conclusions reached etc. is entirely that of the Author. The publisher is not responsible for them, whatsoever.]

All rights reserved. No part of this book may be reproduced, stored in a retrieval system, or transmitted in any form or by any means, electronic, mechanical, photocopying, recording or otherwise, in part or as whole without the prior written permission of the publisher.

All Export rights of this book vest exclusively with Aman Publications. Unauthorised export is a violation of Copyright Law and is subject to legal action.

First Published – 2011

ISBN–978-81–920935–6-7

© Publisher

Published in an association with **HLDC**, Agra.

SOLE DISTRIBUTOR
JINDAL BOOK SERVICES
LG-4A, Ganpati Bhawan,
4675-B/21, Ansari Road,
Darya Ganj, Delhi - 110002

Jacket Designed by :
S.M. Graphics

Printed by:
Sachin Printers, Delhi, India

Preface

Leadership skills are important for managing services, departments and operations at hotels. Hospitality management is the phrase used to describe the education and skill set needed to pursue a career where hospitality is key—hotels, restaurants, casinos, museums, airports, institutional dining services, conventions, conferences, amusement parks, weddings, and so forth. A degree or certificate in hospitality management will prepare you for a career as a hotelier on the front lines, behind the scenes or at top-level industry events. Hospitality management is big business and you must be service-oriented to succeed. Hospitality management, also known as hotel administration, is a career path that warrants its own academic degree programme covering topics such as food safety, nutrition, hotel and restaurant marketing and merchandising, institutional purchasing and cost control, and hospitality supervision.

The supervisors can be found at all levels of management. A supervisor can be a first-line supervisor who has no management positions reporting to them, or it can be the CEO who has every level of management under them! Supervisors ensure that the goals are met and the day-to-day objectives are passed down to the managers and operators beneath them. In this case, the term supervisor is simply a term used to identify 'your boss'.

We hope this text book meets its intended purpose as a practical resource, and serve as a vehicle for promoting the professionalism of this important segment of the Hospitality Industry.

VIKRAM JAIN

HERITAGE

LEARNING & DEVELOPMENT CENTER

Heritage Learning and Development Centre (HLDC) is an extended arm of Heritage Institute of Hotel & Tourism (HIHT). Heritage Institute of Hotel & Tourism is an Institute of excellence of the upcoming chain of Management Institutes, founded by D. K. Singh, President. At HIHT, our endeavour is to take education to the higher domains of never ending success. Heritage Institute of Hotel & Tourism provides the best possible infrastructure for pursuing best quality Hotel Management Education. HIHT has three campuses Agra, Shimla and Goa and proposed campuses at Kolkata, Pune, and Singapore.

In the modern era, Hospitality Industry is a reality, fighting for extremely challenging phase and getting into a stability mode. There are SMILES everywhere and this is relatively controlled and guarded, a sign of maturing and learning of Hospitality, which is cyclic in nature. The Hospitality Industry reflects a bright future. Earlier days, hospitality was synonymous with only hotel industry, but today this industry holds its important place with tourism. Hospitality academic in India is still in its nascent stage when compared to the west.

HLDC has been developed through the inputs from the industry and experts from the academics. This panel of experts have gone through the book and made suggestions which were incorporated. Every attempt has been made to thoroughly cover the day to day problems faced in the profession. In this field, as in most any other, it is prudent to remember the old adage, actions speak louder than words. The information given in this book makes the students fit for the industry. It provides about technical skills, personality and soft skills and ability to think and make decision.

This book is designed and presented in an easy to read and easy to understand format. It will be beneficial to both aspiring professionals and those already in the industry.

We hope this text book meets its intended purpose as a practical resource, and serve as a vehicle for promoting the professionalism of this important segment of the Hospitality Industry.

Contents

1

Basic Overview of Supervision

Supervision is the activity carried out by supervisors to oversee the productivity and progress of employees who report directly to the supervisors. For example, first-level supervisors supervise entry-level employees. Depending on the size of the organisation, middle-managers supervise first-level supervisors, chief executives supervise middle-managers, etc. Supervision is a management activity and supervisors have a management role in the organisation. Occasionally, writers will interchange "leadership" and "supervision". Both activities are closely related. Supervision requires leadership. Leadership does not necessarily have to involve supervision.

Translating military terms into a civilian resume is often one of the most confounding processes for a transitioning soldier, especially when it comes to levels of leadership. The terms *"supervisor"*, *"manager"*, and *"team leader"* are often used to describe the same position. Going in search of solid definitions is not easy.

The point of civilianising your resume is to give an honest picture of your experience, one that a civilian employer will recognise. To overstate your position may cause a potential employer to distrust you. To understate your experience will hurt your chances for career opportunities.

There seems to be few absolute authorities when it comes to defining these roles. However, if you are going to title yourself in your resume, you should be able to offer a definition of that leadership title that supports your translation. The management hierarchy may be confusing, but you need to be clear in your own mind in order to accurately explain your position.

The three terms *"manager"*, *"team leader"*, and *"supervisor"* are confusing because they are somewhat inclusive, but they are not necessarily interchangeable. If used incorrectly or ambiguously during the job search process, the user can be perceived either as unqualified or trying to misrepresent their true position. Managers are individuals who direct, supervise, operate, or control a business. Their functions include planning, organising, directing, coordinating, and supervising personnel and activities within a business or organisation. Management is best described in terms of *levels of management.*

First are the lower levels of management that are referred to as *team leaders* or *first line supervisors.* This is the level often referred to as *operations management*. This is the largest level of management. Many managers believe it to be the most satisfying because this is where the service is provided or the product is produced. *Team leaders* and *First Line Supervisors* plan, organise, supervise, direct and coordinate personnel and activities and make decisions about daily operations of the organisation. These managers usually need more technical skills than middle or upper level managers.

Middle Managers are a step removed from the daily or technical operations. They participate in the same activities as the *First Line Supervisors*, however, the preponderance of their time shifts from supervision of the workforce to planning, organising, and coordinating future activities. *Middle Managers* spend a lot of time with contingency planning and making decisions that effect more people than the F*irst Line Supervisors*. They are given greater responsibilities in goal setting, establishing budgetary needs, human resource development and coordination of various activities within the organisation.

As a *Middle Manager*, they may be responsible for monitoring and evaluating *first line supervisors* and *team leaders*. But as you may have guessed, the further away from the daily operations these managers are, the more managerial skills are needed, education becomes more important versus the hands-on technical skills. Finally, we have upper level or *Top Level Managers*. Managers at this level must have long-range focus. They must have a vision of where the organisation is headed and how it is going to get there. Planning at this level consists of strategic planning and decision-making that affects most, if not all, of the activities and personnel within the organisation.

Top Level Managers usually spend very little time on the daily details of operations; therefore, they require little or no technical skills. They have low and mid-level managers functioning under them to handle the technical end of the operations. However, extensive managerial experience and/or training become a must. Higher or specific education often becomes a nonnegotiable requirement for this level of management.

In general, supervisors can be found at all levels of management. A supervisor can be a first-line supervisor who has no management positions reporting to them, or it can be the CEO who has every level of management under them! *Supervisors* ensure that the goals are met and the day-to-day objectives are passed down to the managers and operators beneath them. In this case, the term supervisor is simply a term used to identify *'your boss'*.

SUPERVISON IN THE HUMAN SERVICES

The immediate roots of what we have come to know as supervision in the human services lie in the development of social work and casework. For example, in the concern for the needs of clients; and the taking up of ideas and practices that owe much to the emergence of psychoanalysis. However, to make sense of supervision it is necessary to look to the various forms of apprenticeship that have existed in different societies.

In ancient China, Africa and Europe, for example, there are numerous examples of people new to a craft or activity having to reveal their work to, and explore it with, masters or mistresses i.e. those recognised as skilled and wise. This process of being attached to an expert, of 'learning through doing' allows the novice to gain knowledge, skill and commitment. It also enables them to enter into a particular 'community of practice' such as tailoring or midwifery. By spending time with practitioners, by 'looking over their shoulders', taking part in the routines and practices associated with the trade or activity, we become full members of the community of practice.

Overseeing

Supervision can be found in the growth of charitable social agencies in Europe and North America during the nineteenth century. It involved the recruitment, organisation and oversight of a large number of volunteers and, later, paid workers. The volunteers were commonly known as 'visitors'. Their task was to call on a small number of families to offer advice and support. The main concern was to foster self help, and the adoption of 'healthy' habits and behaviours.

In addition, visitors were also often in a position to access limited funds via their agencies, although such monies were only given after a careful investigation of the family's circumstances.

In other words, a decision had to be made as to whether they were 'deserving'. The person assigning cases, organising work and taking decisions on behalf of the agency was basically an 'overseer' - and hence the growing use of the term 'supervisor'. As Peters has pointed out, traditionally, part of the overseer's job was to ensure that work was done well and to standard. This can be viewed as an administrative task.

The hierarchical position of the supervisor (or paid agent) was revealed:

> While the 'paid agent' acted as supervisor to the volunteer visitor, the paid agent 'supervisor' was himself supervised by the district committee, which had ultimate authority for case decisions... The paid agent supervisor was then in a middle-management position, as is true of supervisors today - supervising the direct service worker but themselves under the authority of the agency administrators.

It is this hierarchical and managerial idea of supervision that tends to permeate much of the literature in social work.

Kadushin's Model

It is at this point that Alfred Kadushin's discussion of supervision in social work becomes helpful. He goes back to earlier commentators such as John Dawson who stated the functions of supervision in the following terms:

Administrative - the promotion and maintenance of good standards of work, co-ordination of practice with policies of administration, the assurance of an efficient and smooth-running office;

Educational - the educational development of each individual worker on the staff in a manner calculated to evoke her fully to realise her possibilities of usefulness; and

Supportive - the maintenance of harmonious working relationships, the cultivation of esprit de corps.

It is a short step to translate these concerns into the current language of the 'learning organisation'. As Salaman argues, managers must have a concern for both performance and learning.

> The essentially *managerial* aspects of managers' work is their responsibility for monitoring and improving the work of others; their *managerial* effectiveness is determined by their capacity to improve the work of others. if managers are not able to make this contribution, then what value are they adding? The only ultimate justification of managers' existence is the improvement of the work of their subordinates. If managers fail in this way they fail as managers.

In this way managers are expect to develop relationships and environments that enable people to work together and respond to change. Such 'joint performance' involves having common goals, common values, the right structures, and continuing training and development.

Administrative Supervision

Kadushin tightens up on Dawson's formulation and presents his understanding of the three elements in terms of the primary problem and the primary goal. In administrative supervision the primary problem is concerned with the correct, effective and appropriate implementation of agency policies and procedures. The primary goal is to ensure adherence to policy and procedure. The supervisor has been given authority by the agency to oversee the work of the supervisee. This carries the responsibility:

> ... both to *ensure* that agency policy is implemented - which implies a controlling function - and a parallel responsibility to *enable* supervisees to work to the best of their ability.

It also entails a responsibility not to lose touch with the rationale for the agency - 'to provide a first-class service for people who need it'.

Educational Supervision

In educational supervision the primary problem for Kadushin is worker ignorance and/or ineptitude regarding the knowledge, attitude and skills required to do the job. The primary goal is to dispel ignorance and upgrade skill. The classic process involved with this task is to encourage reflection on, and exploration of the work. Supervisees may be helped to:

Understand the client better;

— Become more aware of their own reactions and responses to the client;

— Understand the dynamics of how they and their client are interacting;

— Look at how they intervened and the consequences of their interventions;

— Explore other ways of working with this an other similar client situations

Supportive Supervision

In supportive supervision the primary problem is worker morale and job satisfaction. The primary goal is to improve morale and job satisfaction. Workers are seen as facing a variety of job-related stresses which, unless they have help to deal with them, could seriously affect their work and lead to a less than satisfactory service to clients. For the worker there is ultimately the problem of 'burnout'.

Kadushin argues that the other two forms of supervision focus on instrumental needs, whereas supportive supervision is concerned with expressive needs.

> The supervisor seeks to prevent the development of potentially stressful situations, removes the worker from stress, reduces stress impinging on the worker, and helps her adjust to stress. The supervisor is available and approachable, communicates confidence in the worker, provides perspective, excuses failure when appropriate, sanctions and shares responsibility for different decisions, provides opportunities for independent functioning and for probable success in task achievement.

Having mapped out Kadushin's model it is now possible to look at some of the different foci that can be attributed to supervision. For example, Hawkins and Shohet list 10 different foci and then categorise them in relation to Kadushin's elements.

Primary Foci

— To provide a regular space for the supervisees to reflect upon the *content* and *process* of their work Educational

— To develop understanding and skills within the work Educational
— To receive information and another perspective concerning one's work Educational/Supportive
— To receive both content and process feedback Educational/Supportive
— To be validated and supported both as a person and as a worker Supportive
— To ensure that as a person and as a worker one is not left to carry unnecessarily difficulties, problems and projections alone Supportive
— To have space to explore and express personal distress, restimulation, transference or counter-transference that may be brought up by the work Administrative
— To plan and utilise their *personal* and *professional* resources better Administrative
— To be pro-active rather than reactive Administrative
— To ensure quality of work Administrative/Supportive

Hawkins and Shohet suggest that foci one and two could be seen as educational; foci three and four as educational/supportive; foci five and six as supportive; foci seven to nine as administative/supportive and ten as administrative.

Professional Supervision

The most common distinction is that the manager's first point of reference has to be the interest of the organisation or agency, while the nonmanagerial supervisor looks to the development of the worker. Sometimes this is reduced to the difference between administrative and educational supervision. One version argues that managers should not be concerned with educational supervision; and consultant supervisors should only focus on education and support. There is some truth in portraying the primary responsibilities in this way - but it would be very misleading to leave it there. Kadushin argues that management supervision involves all three categories. Both 'managerial' and 'nonmanagerial' supervisors share larger responsibilities - to the client group and to other professionals; and that both look to the development of the worker.

Psychoanalysis and Counselling

Some of the confusion around supposed differences arises from the roots of consultant, nonmanagerial or professional supervision. Its development has, arguably, owed much to the emergence of psychoanalysis and counselling. In the case of the former, practice, supervision, teaching and personal analysis have formed the central elements of training since the 1920s.

Trainee supervision can be contrasted with practitioner supervision. The latter is addressed to established workers. Some writers, such as Page and Wosket, claim that there are many differences between the focus in supervision of trainees, and that of established practitioners. The former are more likely to be concerned with issues of technique, boundary, understanding the material clients' bring, and dealing with personal feelings of anxiety. 'The experienced practitioner is more likely to be concerned with teasing out relationship dynamics, choosing intervention options and perhaps dealing with feelings of frustration and boredom towards clients'.

The demand for 'practitioner supervision' in counselling can be seen as a key factor in the spread of nonmanagerial or consultant supervision. By the early 1950s, with the 'coming of age' of the profession, there was a substantial growth 'in the proportion of practitioners with significant experience', many of whom valued, 'having a fellow practitioner to act in a consultative capacity'. This linking of consultant supervision with the development of counselling is significant.

The form that supervision takes may well mirror or adopt ways of working from the host profession. Thus, a counsellor supervisor may draw heavily on the theory and practice of a counselling model and apply this to supervision. A psycho-dynamic supervisor would interpret the material being presented and use an awareness of the relationship dynamics between himself and the counsellor in supervision as a means of supervising. A client-centred supervisor would be concerned to communicate the core conditions of acceptance, respect and genuiness to her supervisee.

We now can begin to appreciate why many of the arguments and questions around supervision can become confusing. Contrasts between managerial and consultant supervision, for example, inevitably focus on the managerial element. Yet those involved may well be drawing on very different models and sets of understandings. The debate may be between a psycho-dynamic and a task orientation! This drawing upon from psycho-dynamic and counselling can also add to the common slippage from supervision into therapy or 'working with'.

The first thing to say here is that it may well be appropriate for us as supervisors to change the focus of the session from 'supervision' to 'counselling'. The situation may demand it - and we have what may be described as a 'counselling interlude'. However, there are two particular dangers: we may slip into a different framework without being aware of it; and, further, even where the shift is conscious, it may not be appropriate.

There can also be confusion between *shifting the* frame of reference and *drawing upon* insights from a particular field. It may be that to properly approach a question that has arisen in workers' practice we need to attend to their emotional and psychological lives. Here we may draw upon, for example, psycho-dynamic insights, to work with supervisees to enhance the quality of their interactions with clients. This does not entail moving beyond a supervisor's frame of reference. The focus remains on the enhancement of practice.

Clients, Professionals and the Community

Clients at the centre. It is easy to fall into the trap of viewing changes in the individual supervisee as the central goal of the process. It is not difficult to understand how this happens. As we have seen, in supervision we draw on understandings and ways of working that we have developed in other settings. The most obvious of these are 'counselling' and other one-to-one relationships. Yet, as Kadushin puts it in relation to managerial supervision, 'The supervisor's ultimate objective is to deliver to agency clients the best possible service, both quantitatively and qualitatively, in accordance with agency policies and procedures'. The same applies to consultant or nonmanagerial supervision:

The responsibility of the supervisor to protect the interests of the client emerges as a central component of trainee supervision. Attention to client welfare is equally important... in practitioner supervision. The British Association of Counselling makes the point unambiguously: 'The primary purpose of supervision is to protect the best interests of the client'. Change in supervisees is fostered for a purpose - the enhancement of the service they provide for their clients. However, in considering this we also have to take into account what may be in the interests of the community as a whole.

Accountability to the wider community. In the well known phrase of C. Wright Mills - there are considerable dangers in seeing private troubles merely as troubles - and not as public issues (and vice versa). There is always the danger that we 'slip past structure to focus on isolated situations..., a tendency for problems to be considered as the problems of individuals'.

As practitioners and supervisors we have to balance the needs and wishes of the individual with considerations of those of others in the community. There will be times when what may be identified as being in the interest of the client seriously affects the rights and lives of others. The tensions can be quickly seen if we examine the four basic or first order principles identified by Sarah Banks as central to social work:

— Respect for and promotion of individuals' rights to self determination.
— Promotion of welfare or well-being
— Equality
— Distributive justice.

As supervisors we may have to remind supervisees of the requirement to consider the extent to which a course of action they are pursuing leads to human flourishing, promotes equality or whether they are 'distributing public resources according to certain criteria based variously on rights, dessert and need'. In a similar fashion we have to reflect on our actions as supervisors. Being part of a community of practice. There are likely to be endless arguments about considerations such as these - especially when they are thought about in relation to specific cases and situations.

Managerial supervisors, as members of the profession or community of practice, have a duty to consider the appropriate standards and codes, the main way that they do this is via the policies and practices of the agency. On the other hand, while nonmanagerial or consultant supervisors may be contracted by the supervisee, their authority comes from their membership of the community of practice. Their concern for the service offered to clients is fed through a set of shared understandings concerning what constitutes 'good practice'. In other words, at certain points in the supervision process they may be required to represent that constitutes acceptable behaviour or good practice.

Professional supervisors act on behalf of the community of practice of which they are members. They should have a concern with the quality of service offered and the needs of the wider community. This links back to the way that Proctor redefined Kadushin's administrative category as 'normative'. If we were to adjust Kadushin's definition it would read something like the following:

The primary problem in administrative supervision is concerned with the quality of the supervisee's practice in respect of professional standard and ethics The primary goal is to ensure adherence to these standards.

In other words, so called 'nonmanagerial' supervisors have an administrative responsibility. Where workers consistently fail to live up to these standards or present a danger to clients they have a responsibility to act. This could take the form of them discouraging the supervisee from practice, or of reporting matters to the appropriate professional body. Managerial supervisors also look to professional concerns and to the interests of clients and the wider community, but they do so through the framework of agency policies and procedures.

Training Programme to Supervisor

At this point it may be useful to reflect more fully on the role of the supervisor within professional training programmes such as those involved with informal and community education. For the professional or nonmanagerial supervisor within a training programme the lines of their authority are fairly clear. They act on behalf of the profession or community of practice.

Trainees within programmes are having to develop, and provide evidence concerning, their work so that they may be recognised as qualified to join the professional community. Supervisors agree to provide a certain number of sessions and an assessment of supervisees' abilities for the training provider. The training provider, in turn, is accredited act for the profession by a relevant professional body.

A supervisor may also hold some form of line-managerial responsibility for the worker. In their supervision of the worker they will, thus, want to represent the interests of the agency and safeguard the quality of service offered to the agency's clientele. At the same time their involvement within the training programme highlights their responsibility to the community of practice or profession. Perhaps the best way of representing this is as a dual line of authority - to the profession and to the agency.

2

Supervision in Workplace

Poor supervision in a workplace is among the primary obstacles to achieving potential successes by a business. After all, employees, no matter their task, must have the proper instruction and training to ensure that they are doing their jobs correctly, and with minimal risk of error or injury. After the initial training has been completed, supervision remains necessary for continuing skill and knowledge development among employees. It is for this reason that many businesses today refer to their supervisors as coaches.

When a company has poor supervision, there is not enough responsibility for taking action for the prevention of problems, mistakes, accidents, and injuries. Poor supervision removes a very important part of the employee support process, eliminating the opportunity for reference, learning, and safety. Poor supervision also opens the door for unethical behaviours within a company. With poor supervision, employees commonly feel that their work is not valued by the company, and loyalty is difficult to form – if it forms at all.

Without loyalty, employees are more likely to deviate from acceptable business practices. Such activities can include theft, decreased employee effort, using equipment without authorisation, and falsifying documents, among other things. Of course, poor supervision doesn't only mean that there isn't enough supervision, but can also be the exact opposite, where there is too much supervision. When employees feel as though they are being too heavily watched and policed, they get the feeling that the company doesn't trust or respect them. This increases tension in the workplace and decreases overall employee morale.

To avoid poor supervision in your business, you should consider supervisors not necessarily to be rule enforcers, but instead, they should be employee support people. They are the individuals who can assist employees when their work can be improved through different techniques. They impart safety knowledge and are the people to whom employees can come if they have questions and concerns about their tasks.

A good supervisor should be approachable and a good people-person who knows the different equipment and jobs required by the employees, and is willing to help employees achieve. If a supervisor is not present enough, or is too overbearing, then the reaction from employees will only be fear, resentment, and displeasure in their work. The productivity will not be as good, and the employee turnover will increase.

In a company that intends to maximise its performance and profits, a quality supervisory team should be employed and trained to ensure the very finest results from their individual employee groups. These supervisors should have their own support system, and their importance should be made very clear, to ensure the highest degree of productivity.

An employee is a supervisor if they have the power and authority to do the following actions:

— Give instructions and/or orders to subordinates.

— Be held responsible for the work and actions of other employees.

— Administer discipline and penalties.

If an employee cannot do all of the above, legally he is probably not a supervisor, but in some other category, such as lead hand. A supervisor is first and foremost a gang boss whose main responsibility is to ensure that a group of subordinates get out the assigned amount of production, when they are supposed to do it and within acceptable levels of quality, costs and safety.

A Supervisor is responsible for the productivity and actions of a small group of employees. The Supervisor has several manager like roles, responsibilities, and powers. Two of the key differences between a Supervisor and a Manager are:

(1) the Supervisor does not typically have "hire and fire" authority, and

(2) the Supervisor does not have budget authority.

Lacking "hire and fire" authority means that a Supervisor may not recruit the employees working in the Supervisor's group nor does the Supervisor have the authority to terminate an employee. The Supervisor may participate in the hiring process as part of interviewing and assessing candidates but the actual hiring authority rests in the hands of a Human Resource Manager. The Supervisor may recommend to management that a particular employee be terminated and the Supervisor may be the one who documents the behaviours leading to the recommendation but the actual firing authority rests in the hands of a Manager.

Lacking budget authority means that a Supervisor is provided a budget developed by management within which constraints the Supervisor is expected to provide a productive environment for the employees of the Supervisor's work group. A Supervisor will usually have the authority to make purchases within specified limits. A Supervisor is also given the power to approve work hours and other payroll issues. Normally, budget affecting requests such as travel will require not only the Supervisor's approval but the approval of one or more layers of management.

As a member of management, a supervisor's main job is more concerned with orchestrating and controlling work rather than performing it directly. The role of the supervisor in a factory setting is quite new, starting about two hundred years ago. At the start of the Industrial Revolution, the factory owners realised that they needed foremen who could force the unskilled and uneducated factory workers into changing their work habits to fit the new factory system.

The uneducated and unskilled workers, who were drawn in from the countryside, needed to learn a whole new way of existence, a life that made the hourly wage and the factory whistle the central part of their waking life. It was the foreman's job to force the workers to stay at their machines for their entire twelve to fourteen hour shifts and not go around socialising with whomever they met. Brutal discipline was combined with starvation wages to force the workers into accepting the modern factory system.

For instance, in England when the factory whistle blew in the morning, the factory gates were locked and all the tardy workers were not allowed in until lunchtime. They were then fined a further four hours pay. Life and work in the early factory towns did not improve the life of the workers; that took some time in coming. At the time of Charles Dickens, the life expectancy in Britain dropped to seventeen years compared to a life expectancy of nineteen for the citizens of the Roman Empire. The skilled tradesmen, banded together in craft unions, used their knowledge and limited numbers to retain a level of independence and better conditions that, to some degree, remains today.

Supervisor's Responsibilities

A supervisor in the workplace has four distinctly separate sets of responsibilities. The supervisor's first duty is to represent management and the company. It is the supervisor's job to organise his/her department and employees, visualise future impacts and needs, energise the employees to get their tasks done and supervise their work ensuring that the productivity and quality standards are met. To ensure that this is done, the supervisor makes certain that his employees have the training, the tools and the material that they need to carry out their duties.

Another important part of the job is to act as a middleman and buffer between the employees who actually do the job and the rest of the organisation. The supervisor makes sure that his employees' pay is correct, their vacation pay arrives on time and they receive proper care if they get injured on the job. The supervisor also has legal responsibilities to ensure that his area of responsibility is free of safety violations, all employees received proper training and that all human rights are upheld.

Supervisors are also responsible for the health and safety of all their subordinates and to ensure that they work in a harassment-free environment. It is also the supervisor's responsibility to develop all the potential leaders that work under him so that the company can identify and place all the employees who demonstrate that they have the interest and abilities to be promoted or transferred to better positions.

Supervisors are usually responsible for the progress and productivity of their employees, whether the supervisor is an executive supervising a middle manager or a first-time supervisor supervising a new employee. Note that in some types of organisations, e.g., a matrix organisation, the supervisor attends solely to the responsibilities of the supervisoral role.

However, in many organisations, the supervisor is responsible not only for supervisoral responsibilities, but also for product-line responsibilities, that is, to get a product or service out the door. Products and services generate revenue. Consequently, the role of supervision sometimes takes a "background" role to the product-line role.

Human Resources Department

Note that if the organisation is large enough, the supervisor is fortunate to have a staff department, e.g., Human Resources (HR) Department, that directs or supports many of the activities carried out by supervisors. The supervisor still carries out the supervisory responsibilities, but HR is a tremendous help.

For example, HR guides and supports activities in staffing, development and management of personnel policies and records, training and development, performance appraisals and performance problems, career counselling, organisation development, etc. HR provides this help and ensures that all activities conform to current rules and regulations.

Policies and Procedures

The supervisor is usually responsible to ensure that employees follow the organisation's policies and procedures, e.g., for sick time, personal leave, overtime, contact with the media or press, confidentiality about organisation information, etc. Concurrently, the supervisor must follow policies and procedures for carrying out supervisory responsibilities, e.g., policies and procedures for hiring, firing, promotions.

Employees

Supervisors regularly review the needs of their employees. Consequently, they're often the first to notice the need for a new position in the organisation. In this case, the supervisor opens a new role by getting authorisation from upper management. This often requires communication and justification for funds to fill the new position. The supervisor reviews advertisements for job candidates, reviews resumes and conducts interviews.

The supervisor recommends who should be hired from among job candidates and ensures a job offer is made to the most suitable candidate. There's usually a great deal of paperwork, e.g., a job application, starting a personnel file, providing an employee manual, salary and tax forms, etc. Finally, the supervisor must ensure the new employee has adequate facilities, e.g., desk, computer, office supplies, etc.

Employee Training

Supervisors ensure new employees are oriented to the organisation, its policies, facilities, etc. They develop training plans with employees to ensure employees have the necessary expertise to carry out their jobs. They provide ongoing guidance to employees, often in the forms of ongoing coaching and counselling. Supervisors often provide career counselling, as well, to help employees develop and advance in their careers.

Employee Performance

Supervisors ensure that job descriptions accurately record the primary responsibilities, qualifications and terms for each job role in their group. They set performance standards for tasks, jobs and roles of their employees. They ensure employees have appropriate and realistic job goals. They provide ongoing feedback about the employee's performance. They conduct performance appraisals on a regular basis, including assessing how the employee has performed and what they can do to improve in their jobs. They develop performance improvement plans if an employee's performance is not adequate. In addition, supervisors provide rewards for employee accomplishments.

Organisational Supervision

Most people will agree on what key knowledge, skills and abilities are required to drive a car — this is not the case with supervisor training. Introductory courses, workshops and seminars on supervision can include a wide range of topics and depend very much on what the designer of the training programme believes supervisors should know. These beliefs can vary widely, particularly because: a) trainers have varying opinions about roles of supervisors; and b) the nature of today's workplace is changing to include more, eg, self-managed teams, emphasis on leadership, diversity management, performance management, etc.

There are often misunderstandings about the role of supervisors, for example, people mistakenly believe that supervision occurs only with entry-level workers. This belief is incorrect. Chief Executive Officers are supervisors of Chief Financial Officers, and middle-line managers are supervisors of first-line managers, etc. Also, trainers can forget that supervisors are seldom only responsible for supervision. Too often, supervision is carried out "in the background", secondary to getting a product or service out the door. Consequently, supervisory training programmes sometimes neglect to include key skills, such as handling burnout, stress management, time management, etc.

Marginal Performer

Federal agencies cannot afford employees who are performing their duties less than fully successfully. Government wide regulations recommend that agencies provide assistance whenever performance becomes marginally successful. However, unlike the regulations for dealing with employees who are *Unacceptable*, the regulations do not specify what should be done for marginal performers.

Reasons for addressing marginal performance. Good supervisors do not allow marginal performance to continue, for these reasons:

— When employees' performance deteriorates, they often perform at the marginal level for a time before dropping to *Unacceptable*. Catching and addressing poor performance before it becomes *Unacceptable* is an easier and more effective way of dealing with performance problems.

— If supervisors talk with employees when performance first becomes marginal, the discussions may serve as a "wake-up call." When employees first slip into marginal performance, they are more likely to be open to discussing what needs to be done to improve performance.

— Supervisors can help employees improve without the negative consequences of threatening their jobs. Employees can concentrate on building necessary skills without worrying about possible unemployment at the end of the performance improvement period.

— By addressing performance problems, supervisors signal to all employees that the organisation does not tolerate poor performance.

Here are a few tips for assisting marginal performers. In addition to following these tips, supervisors should also remember to check with their Human Resources Office to see if their agency has a formal process for addressing marginal performance.

— *Clear communication*: Supervisors must communicate clear performance standards and expectations. They should take time to look at the existing performance standards and make some changes if the standards don't really communicate their expectations. If employees don't understand what is expected, it is very hard — sometimes impossible — for them to meet those expectations.

— *Frequent feedback*: Positive, constructive feedback from supervisors, given whenever needed, is crucial to ensuring that employees know what they've done right and what needs improvement. Feedback should be specific, meaningful, and timely.

— *Increased supervision*: Marginal employees often require more direction. Supervisors should work more closely with them, while understanding that the goal is for employees to work competently and independently.

— *Positive reinforcement*: Recognise good performance. Recognising marginal employees when they do something correctly is another way of clarifying expectations and providing positive reinforcement. Recognising good performance increases the likelihood that employees will repeat the performance.

— *Mentoring*: Have an outstanding employee serve as a mentor for the marginal performer. In this way, supervisors provide a model of desired performance.

— *Training*: In some situations, marginal employees need training because they lack the skills to perform at the *Fully Successful* level. Training can include formal classroom sessions, on-the-job training, and automated training aids.

— *Checklists*: Often employees performing at the marginal level require extra assistance in setting priorities and remembering procedures. Checklists can sometimes help employees stay focused on a task and organise their work.

Employee Performance Standards

A performance standard is a management-approved expression of the performance threshold(s), requirement(s), or expectation(s) that must be met to be appraised at a particular level of performance. A Fully Successful (or equivalent) standard must be established for each critical element and included in the employee performance plan. If other levels of performance are used by the appraisal programme, writing standards for those levels and including them in the performance plan is not required by is encouraged so that employees will know what they have to do to meet standards higher than Fully Successful.

Performance standards should be objective, measurable, realistic, and stated clearly in writing (or otherwise recorded). The standards should be written in terms of specific measurers that will be used to appraise performance. In order to develop specific measurers, you first must determine the general measure(s) that are important for each element. General measurers used to measure employee performance include the following:

— Quality address how well the work is performed and/or how accurate or how effective the final product is. Quality refers to accuracy, appearance, usefulness, or effectiveness.

— Quantity addresses how much work is produced. A quantity measure can be expressed as an error rate, such as number ore percentage of errors allowable per unit of work, or as a general result to be achieved. When a quality or quantity standard is set, the Fully Successful standard should be high enough to be challenging but not so high that it is not really achievable.

— Timeliness addresses how quickly, when or by what date the work is produced. The most common error made in setting timeliness standards is to allow no margin for error. As with other standards, timeliness standards should be set realistically in view of other performance requirements and needs of the organisation.

— Cost-Effectiveness addresses dollar savings to the Government or working within a budget. Standards that address cost-effectiveness should be based on specific resource levels (money, personnel, or time) that generally can be documented and measured in agencies' annual fiscal year budgets. Cost-effectiveness standards may include such aspects of performance as maintaining or reducing unit costs, reducing the time it takes to produce a product or service, or reducing waste.

Once you've decided which general measures are important, you can develop specific measurers. It is these specific measures that will be included in the standard. To develop specific measure(s) for each element, you must determine how you would measure the quantity, quality, timeliness, and/or cost-effectiveness of the element. If it can be measured with numbers, clearly define those numbers. If performance only can be described, clarify who would be the best judge to appraise the work and what factors they would look for.

Once you've established the specific measures that apply to the elements, you can begin to write the standards. Before writing the Fully Successful standard, you must know the number of levels that your appraisal programme uses to appraise elements.

For example, if you are under an appraisal programme that uses two levels to appraise elements, the Fully Successful standard would describe a single point of performance, above which is Fully Successful, and below which is Unacceptable. If, however, your appraisal programme uses five levels to appraise elements, you would describe the Fully Successful standard as a range, above which is higher than Fully Successful, and below which would be Minimally Successful.

If a specific measure for an element is numeric, for example, you would list the units to be tracked and determine the range of numbers that represents Fully Successful performance. If the specific measure is descriptive, you would identify the judge, list the factors that the judge would look for, and determine what he or she would see or report that verifies that Fully Successful performance for that element had been met.

Guidance and technical assistance

Fully Successful Standard in an appraisal programme that appraises elements at five levels:

— No more than 3-8% errors per quarter, as determined by the supervisor.

— At least 60-80% of customers agree that the employee is willing to assist and that the information they receive is helpful.

— Employee initially responds to customer requests for assistance within at least 1-8 working hours from receipt of request.

Team participation

Fully Successful Standard in an appraisal programme that appraises elements at five levels:

The supervisor and team members are satisfied that the incumbent:

— Usually assumes an appropriate amount of work/ responsibility for group projects;

— Typically demonstrates a willingness to assume other responsibilities as needed; and

— Generally shares knowledge of office procedures/ equipment with other members of the team.

Analytical results and specifications

Fully Successful Standard in an appraisal programme that appraises elements at five levels:

The Research Manager is routinely satisfied that:

— The method measures that appropriate variable.

— The results are relevant.

— The method is scientifically sound.
— There is a well-written protocol.
— The method is accurate, precise, reproducible, fast, and cost-effective.

Consensus

One of the conditions necessary for successful team work is team members' ability to make decisions and solve problems as a group. Some of the most effective decision-making processes include building consensus.

Consensus means coming to an agreement. Creating consensus in a team setting means finding a proposal acceptable enough that all team members can support it, with no member opposing it. Consensus includes:

— pooling opinions;
— listening effectively;
— discussing ideas and differences;
— not getting all you want; and
— coming to an agreement that everyone "can live with."

Consensus is not:

— a unanimous vote;
— majority or minority rule;
— one-person rule; or
— bargaining.

Teams can reach consensus using formal and informal methods. Highly developed teams may be able to reach consensus informally. However, new teams or groups of employees who are not familiar with each other will need more structured methods to help them build consensus-methods such as brainstorming, multi-voting, and nominal group technique. Brainstorming is a simple and effective method of generating ideas in a group. It begins with a facilitator defining the problem or the topic. Then, each team member suggests ideas-either in turn or as ideas arise-and those ideas are written on a board or flip chart.

Team members should not criticise or evaluate any idea during the brainstorming session. After the team generates the ideas, the group refines the list by asking for explanations, combining ideas, and if necessary, prioritising ideas from most effective to least effective. Multi-voting can reduce a list containing a large number of items to a manageable few. At the beginning of the process, each member gets a number of votes equal to no more than one-half or one-third of the total number of items listed.

Members cast their votes for the items they perceive as best on the list, but may cast only one vote per item. Items receiving votes from half or more of the group are circled. The process repeats, with members casting limited votes for the best of the remaining circled items. The team continues multi-voting until it reduces the list to three to five items.

Nominal group technique is a two-part process that provides a more structured approach than brainstorming or multi-voting. First, the team runs a brainstorming session to generate a list of ideas. Once they have the list, members discuss and clarify the ideas. Then, each member receives small cards to equal a fraction of the number of ideas still on the list.

The members use the cards to vote for the ideas they like the most by recording one idea per card and assigning that idea a rank order, with "1" being the least favourite. The facilitator or team leader gathers the cards and tallies the ranks given to each idea. The idea that has the highest point total is the team's selection.

Formula for Good Performance

Managers play their most important role when they set the stage for good performance. By understanding the factors that contribute to performance, management can focus on those factors to improve the results their employees and organisations achieve. Federal regulations define employee performance as the accomplishment of work assignments or responsibilities. Organisational performance is the accomplishment of organisational goals. To achieve good performance, organisations and employees must have the capacity and the commitment to perform. Written as a formula, this concept can be expressed as:

Performance = Capacity x Commitment

Note that performance is the product of two factors-capacity and commitment. If either one of these factors is zero, the result is zero. In addition, the relationship of capacity to commitment in this equation means that adjustments to either factor will affect performance. Knowing this, managers can analyse various factors of the equation and address those areas that are weak to improve the result of the equation: performance.

Capacity to Perform

In a work setting, the capacity to perform means having available the competencies, the resources, and the opportunity to complete the job. If employees are missing these, the work will not get done and the results will not be achieved. In other words:

Capacity = Competencies x Resources x Opportunity

— *Competencies*: Competencies are sets of measurable skills, knowledge, behaviours, and personal attributes critical to successful performance. Employees must have the right competencies in order to complete a job satisfactorily. Organisational leaders must pay close attention to this factor in the performance equation. They should carefully determine which competencies are important to achieving the results set out in strategic and performance plans so that they can hire the best people for the job, make effective work assignments, and establish individual development plans for employees that focus on the most important competencies.

— *Resources*: Employees must be given the resources they need to do their jobs. A key management responsibility is to ensure employees have a work environment that contains the tools they need to be effective. If employees have all the competencies needed to complete the job, but lack the resources to perform, the job will not get done. For example, customer service representatives who do not have working phones at their desk will not be able to call their customers to ask if their needs were met.

— *Opportunity*: Employees may have the competencies and the resources to do the job, but may never be given the opportunity to perform. For example, a public relations specialist assigned to facilitate public forums will not have the opportunity to perform that assignment if no public forums are held. Supervisors should be aware when situations arise that prevent a competent employee from performing assigned duties well.

Commitment

In a work setting, commitment means, at a minimum,

that an employee agrees to complete assigned work and meet or exceed specific standards of quality, quantity, and timeliness that add value to the organisation and its results. The level of employee commitment to the job is often the key determinant of whether an employee performs marginally or exceeds expectations.

Methods for gaining employee commitment include:

— setting clear goals for employees that require effort to achieve but are reachable;

— showing employees how they fit into the "big picture" of the organisation's mission and how their work helps the organisation accomplish its goals;

— involving employees and their representatives in decision-making processes that affect how the work gets done as well as the quality of work life;

— measuring performance and results using credible measures that employees understand and accept;

— using employee input to develop employee performance plans;

— creating a work climate where employees feel valued; and

— recognising and rewarding—formally and informally—employee achievements.

Obtaining and maintaining employee commitment can be the most challenging factor of the performance formula. But practicing good performance management techniques offers supervisors and managers the ways and means to sustain and improve that commitment and thereby further leverage their employees' capacity to perform.

Performance Management Process

Finally — the data are in and the results are clear:

performance management processes done well are key to creating a productive work climate and retaining good employees!

The performance management processes of planning, monitoring, developing, and rewarding performance surface time and again as critical factors for success. For example, in the 1998-1999 Hay Employee Attitudes Study, "Competing for Talent: Creating A Work Climate to Attract, Motivate and Retain High Performing Employees," the Hay Group compares two groups of employees — those committed to the organisation and those planning to leave. Many of the critical factors affecting employee retention relate to the quality of performance management. These include:

— type of work (planning);

— coaching/feedback from boss (monitoring);

— opportunity to learn new skills (developing);

— training (developing); and

— recognition for a job well done (rewarding).

Leadership

According to Dr. Warren Blank in his book *The 9 Natural Laws of Leadership*, defining leadership is not a simple matter - a leadership strategy that works in one particular situation may not work again at another time under the same conditions. Instead of providing a simple definition, the author presents leadership in terms of nine natural laws that offer an integrated portrait of leadership.

Nine natural laws of leadership:

— A leader has willing followers. No leader exists without gaining the support of others. This first natural law recognises the collegial role of followers.

— Leadership is a field of interaction - a relationship between leaders and followers. Leadership is not a person, a position, or a programme but a relationship that develops when the leader and the follower connect to create one, undivided whole.

— Leadership occurs as an event. Leadership exists as relationships between leaders and followers, with these alliances being transitory events. People who are viewed as great leaders generally have had a series of successful leadership events and work at maintaining a core of loyal followers.

— Leaders use influence beyond formal authority. Managers rely on the influence and authority of their position to get things accomplished. The difference between leaders and managers, according to Blank, is that leaders rely on the influence gained through the web of interactions they have with their followers. Managers rely on institutional authority.

— Leaders operate outside the boundaries of organisationally defined procedures. Managers provide direction while leaders chart direction beyond that prescribed by existing procedures. The author quotes Sun Tzu in *The Art of War*: "Don't follow where the pathway goes, lead instead where there is no path and leave a trail."

— Leadership involves risk and uncertainty. The reality of leadership requires that someone accept the risk that is part of the territory when acting outside the prescribed procedures.

— Not everyone will follow a leader's initiative. This is one of the most critical limits of leadership. No leader, even the best known, such as Abraham Lincoln, Ghandi, or Dr. Martin Luther King, will have the support of all their potential followers.

— Consciousness - information processing - creates leadership. Leaders think differently. They perceive opportunities and ways of overcoming obstacles that others do not. Leadership occurs when a person influences others to recognise his or her direction as useful - when they can sell others on their idea.

Leadership is a self-referral process. Leaders and followers process information from their own subjective, internal frame of reference. Every leader sees the world through his or her specific lenses, and followers identify with a leader because the leader fits the followers' self-referral image of what a leader should be. Compare the nonviolent approach of Dr. Martin Luther King with the cruelty of Adolf Hitler - two completely different leaders with completely different types of followers.

Recruiting and Selecting Employees

As all employers quickly learn, there's a world of difference between a worker who's correctly matched to their job and their organisation, and one who is not. By including, in your comprehensive people strategy, a well-structured recruiting and selection programme. The key to successfully developing such a programme is to follow a proven recruiting process for the positions you need to fill. Resist the temptation to omit steps, because shortcutting the process can shortchange your results.

Develop accurate job descriptions: Your first step is to make sure you have an effective job description for each position in your company. Your job descriptions should reflect careful thought as to the roles the individual will fill, the skill sets they'll need, the personality attributes that are important to completing their tasks, and any relevant experience that would differentiate one applicant from another. This may sound fairly basic, but you'd be surprised at how many small companies fail to develop or maintain updated job descriptions.

Compile a "success profile": In addition to creating job descriptions, it's important to develop a "success profile" of the ideal employee for key positions in your company that are critical to the execution of your business plan. These might include such positions as team leaders, district managers and salespeople. For example, let's say you currently have 20 salespeople. Within that group, you have four that are top performers, 12 that are middle-of-the-road and four that aren't quite making the grade. If you could bump the number of folks in the top group from 20 percent to 33 percent, that could have a dramatic impact on your company's performance.

To accomplish that goal, you need to profile everyone in the sales group to identify any skills and attributes that are common to the top group but missing from the other groups. Using this information, you'll be able to develop a profile to help you select the candidates most likely to succeed in that position. Remember, you can't tell if you've found a match if you're not matching candidates against a specific profile.

Draft the ad, describing the position and the key qualifications required. Although some applicants will ignore these requirements and respond regardless, including this information will help you limit the number of unqualified applicants. Post the ad in the mediums most likely to reach your potential job candidates. Of course, the Internet has become the leading venue for posting job openings, but don't overlook targeted industry publications and local newspapers.

Develop a series of phone-screening questions: Compile a list of suitable questions you can ask over the phone to help you quickly identify qualified candidates and eliminate everyone else. Review the resumes you receive and identify your best candidates. Once you post your ad, you'll start receiving resumes sometimes many more than you anticipated. Knowing what you're looking for in terms of experience, education and skills will help you weed through these resumes quickly and identify potential candidates.

Screen candidates by phone: Once you've narrowed your stack of resumes to a handful of potential applicants, call the candidates and use your phone-screening questions to further narrow the field. Using a consistent set of questions in both this step and your face-to-face interviews will help ensure you're evaluating candidates equally. Select candidates for assessment. Based on the responses to your phone interviews, select the candidates you feel are best qualified for the next step in the process.

Assess your potential candidates for their skills and attributes using a proven assessment tool. A resume and phone interview can only tell you so much about a job applicant, so you'll need a dependable assessment tool to help you analyse the core behavioural traits and cognitive reasoning speed of your applicants. For example, a good test will provide insights as to whether the individual is conscientious or lackadaisical, introverted or extroverted, agreeable or uncompromising, open to new ideas or close-minded, and emotionally stable or anxious and insecure.

The success profile you created for each position will help you determine which behavioural traits are important for that position. For example, you would expect a successful salesperson to be extroverted. On the other hand, someone filling a clerical position might be more introverted. These assessment tests can be administered in person or online. Online testing and submission of results can help you determine whether the applicant should be invited for a personal interview.

Schedule and conduct candidate interviews: Once you've selected candidates based on the previous steps, schedule and conduct the interviews. Use a consistent set of 10 or 12 questions to maintain a structured interview and offer a sound basis for comparing applicants. Select the candidate. Make your selection by matching the best applicant to the profiled job description. Run a background check on the individual to uncover any potential problems not revealed by previous testing and interviews. Make your offer to the candidate. The information you collected during the interview process will provide you with important insights as to starting compensation levels and training needs.

3

Employee Development

Employee development programmes make positive contributions to organisational performance. A more highly-skilled workforce can accomplish more and a supervisor's group can accomplish more as employees gain in experience and knowledge.

Employee Training and Development

Training and development can be initiated for a variety of reasons for an employee or group of employees, e.g:

— When a performance appraisal indicates performance improvement is needed

— To "benchmark" the status of improvement so far in a performance improvement effort

— As part of an overall professional development programme

— As part of succession planning to help an employee be eligible for a planned change in role in the organisation

— To "pilot", or test, the operation of a new performance management system

— To train about a specific topic

Typical Topics of Employee Training

— *Communications:* The increasing diversity of today's workforce brings a wide variety of languages and customs.

— *Computer skills:* Computer skills are becoming a necessity for conducting administrative and office tasks.

— *Customer service:* Increased competition in today's global marketplace makes it critical that employees understand and meet the needs of customers.

— *Diversity:* Diversity training usually includes explanation about how people have different perspectives and views, and includes techniques to value diversity

— *Ethics:* Today's society has increasing expectations about corporate social responsibility. Also, today's diverse workforce brings a wide variety of values and morals to the workplace.

— *Human relations:* The increased stresses of today's workplace can include misunderstandings and conflict. Training can people to get along in the workplace.

— *Quality initiatives:* Initiatives such as Total Quality Management, Quality Circles, benchmarking, etc., require basic training about quality concepts, guidelines and standards for quality, etc.

— *Safety:* Safety training is critical where working with heavy equipment, hazardous chemicals, repetitive activities, etc., but can also be useful with practical advice for avoiding assaults, etc.

— *Sexual harassment:* Sexual harassment training usually includes careful description of the organisation's policies about sexual harassment, especially about what are inappropriate behaviours.

General Benefits

There are numerous sources of on-line information about training and development. Several of these sites (they're listed later on in this library) suggest reasons for supervisors to conduct training among employees. These reasons include:

— Increased job satisfaction and morale among employees

— Increased employee motivation

— Increased efficiencies in processes, resulting in financial gain

— Increased capacity to adopt new technologies and methods

— Increased innovation in strategies and products

— Reduced employee turnover

— Enhanced company image, e.g., conducting ethics training (not a good reason for ethics training!)

— Risk management, e.g., training about sexual harassment, diversity training

Training and Development Purpose

Reasons for emphasizing the growth and development of personnel include

— Creating a pool of readily available and adequate replacements for personnel who may leave or move up in the organisation.

— Enhancing the company's ability to adopt and use advances in technology because of a sufficiently knowledgeable staff.

— Building a more efficient, effective and highly motivated team, which enhances the company's competitive position and improves employee morale.

— Ensuring adequate human resources for expansion into new programmes.

Research has shown specific benefits that a small business receives from training and developing its workers, including:

— Increased productivity.

— Reduced employee turnover.

— Increased efficiency resulting in financial gains.

— Decreased need for supervision.

Employees frequently develop a greater sense of self-worth, dignity and well-being as they become more valuable to the firm and to society. Generally they will receive a greater share of the material gains that result from their increased productivity. These factors give them a sense of satisfaction through the achievement of personal and company goals.

Training Process

The model below traces the steps necessary in the training process:

— Organisational Objectives

— Needs Assessment

— Is There a Gap?

— Training Objectives

— Select the Trainees

— Select the Training Methods and Mode

— Choose a Means of Evaluating

— Administer Training

— Evaluate the Training

Your business should have a clearly defined strategy and set of objectives that direct and drive all the decisions made especially for training decisions. Firms that plan their training process are more successful than those that do not. Most business owners want to succeed, but do not engage in training designs that promise to improve their chances of success. Why? The five reasons most often identified are:

— Time - *Small businesses managers find that time demands do not allow them to train employees.*

— Getting started - *Most small business managers have not practiced training employees. The training process is unfamiliar.*

— Broad expertise - *Managers tend to have broad expertise rather than the specialised skills needed for training and development activities.*

— Lack of trust and openness - *Many managers prefer to keep information to themselves. By doing so they keep information from subordinates and others who could be useful in the training and development process.*

— Skepticism as to the value of the training - *Some small business owners believe the future cannot be predicted or controlled and their efforts, therefore, are best centered on current activities i.e., making money today.*

A well-conceived training programme can help your firm succeed. A programme structured with the company's strategy and objectives in mind has a high probability of improving productivity and other goals that are set in the training mission.

For any business, formulating a training strategy requires addressing a series of questions.

— Who are your customers? Why do they buy from you?

— Who are your competitors? How do they serve the market? What competitive advantages do they enjoy? What parts of the market have they ignored?

— What strengths does the company have? What weaknesses?

— What social trends are emerging that will affect the firm?

The purpose of formulating a training strategy is to answer two relatively simple but vitally important questions: (1) What is our business? and (2) What should our business be? Armed with the answers to these questions and a clear vision of its mission, strategy and objectives, a company can identify its training needs.

Training needs can be assessed by analysing three major human resource areas: the organisation as a whole, the job characteristics and the needs of the individuals. This analysis will provide answers to the following questions:

— Where is training needed?

— What specifically must an employee learn in order to be more productive?

— Who needs to be trained?

Begin by assessing the current status of the company how it does what it does best and the abilities of your employees to do these tasks. This analysis will provide some benchmarks against which the effectiveness of a training programme can be evaluated. Your firm should know where it wants to be in five years from its long-range strategic plan. What you need is a training programme to take your firm from here to there.

Second, consider whether the organisation is financially committed to supporting the training efforts. If not, any attempt to develop a solid training programme will fail. Next, determine exactly where training is needed. It is foolish to implement a companywide training effort without concentrating resources where they are needed most. An internal audit will help point out areas that may benefit from training. Also, a skills inventory can help determine the skills possessed by the employees in general. This inventory will help the organisation determine what skills are available now and what skills are needed for future development.

Also, in today's market-driven economy, you would be remiss not to ask your customers what they like about your business and what areas they think should be improved. In summary, the analysis should focus on the total organisation and should tell you (1) where training is needed and (2) where it will work within the organisation.

Once you have determined where training is needed, concentrate on the content of the programme. Analyse the characteristics of the job based on its description, the written narrative of what the employee actually does. Training based on job descriptions should go into detail about how the job is performed on a task-by-task basis. Actually doing the job will enable you to get a better feel for what is done. Individual employees can be evaluated by comparing their current skill levels or performance to the organisation's performance standards or anticipated needs. Any discrepancies between actual and anticipated skill levels identifies a training need.

Trainees Selection

Once you have decided what training is necessary and where it is needed, the next decision is who should be trained? For a small business, this question is crucial. Training an employee is expensive, especially when he or she leaves your firm for a better job. Therefore, it is important to carefully select who will be trained.

Training programmes should be designed to consider the ability of the employee to learn the material and to use it effectively, and to make the most efficient use of resources possible. It is also important that employees be motivated by the training experience. Employee failure in the programme is not only damaging to the employee but a waste of money as well. Selecting the right trainees is important to the success of the programme.

Training Goals of the Training Programme

The goals of the training programme should relate directly to the needs determined by the assessment process outlined above. Course objectives should clearly state what behaviour or skill will be changed as a result of the training and should relate to the mission and strategic plan of the company. Goals should include milestones to help take the employee from where he or she is today to where the firm wants him or her in the future. Setting goals helps to evaluate the training programme and also to motivate employees. Allowing employees to participate in setting goals increases the probability of success.

Methods of Training

There are two broad types of training available to small businesses: on-the-job and off-the-job techniques. Individual circumstances and the "who," "what" and "why" of your training programme determine which method to use.

On-the-job training is delivered to employees while they perform their regular jobs. In this way, they do not lose time while they are learning. After a plan is developed for what should be taught, employees should be informed of the details. A timetable should be established with periodic evaluations to inform employees about their progress. On-the-job techniques include orientations, job instruction training, apprenticeships, internships and assistantships, job rotation and coaching.

Off-the-job techniques include lectures, special study, films, television conferences or discussions, case studies, role playing, simulation, programmed instruction and laboratory training. Most of these techniques can be used by small businesses although, some may be too costly. Orientations are for new employees. The first several days on the job are crucial in the success of new employees. This point is illustrated by the fact that 60 percent of all employees who quit do so in the first ten days. Orientation training should emphasise the following topics:

— The company's history and mission.

— The key members in the organisation.

— The key members in the department, and how the department helps fulfil the mission of the company.

— Personnel rules and regulations.

Some companies use verbal presentations while others have written presentations. Many small businesses convey these topics in one-on-one orientations. No matter what method is used, it is important that the newcomer understand his or her new place of employment.

Lectures present training material verbally and are used when the goal is to present a great deal of material to many people. It is more cost effective to lecture to a group than to train people individually. Lecturing is one-way communication and as such may not be the most effective way to train. Also, it is hard to ensure that the entire audience understands a topic on the same level; by targeting the average attendee you may undertrain some and lose others. Despite these drawbacks, lecturing is the most cost-effective way of reaching large audiences.

Role playing and simulation are training techniques that attempt to bring realistic decision making situations to the trainee. Likely problems and alternative solutions are presented for discussion. The adage there is no better trainer than experience is exemplified with this type of training. Experienced employees can describe real world experiences, and can help in and learn from developing the solutions to these simulations. This method is cost effective and is used in marketing and management training.

Audiovisual methods such as television, videotapes and films are the most effective means of providing real world conditions and situations in a short time. One advantage is that the presentation is the same no matter how many times it's played. This is not true with lectures, which can change as the speaker is changed or can be influenced by outside constraints. The major flaw with the audiovisual method is that it does not allow for questions and interactions with the speaker, nor does it allow for changes in the presentation for different audiences.

Job rotation involves moving an employee through a series of jobs so he or she can get a good feel for the tasks that are associated with different jobs. It is usually used in training for supervisory positions. The employee learns a little about everything. This is a good strategy for small businesses because of the many jobs an employee may be asked to do.

Apprenticeships develop employees who can do many different tasks. They usually involve several related groups of skills that allow the apprentice to practice a particular trade, and they take place over a long period of time in which the apprentice works for, and with, the senior skilled worker. Apprenticeships are especially appropriate for jobs requiring production skills.

Internships and assistantships are usually a combination of classroom and on-the-job training. They are often used to train prospective managers or marketing personnel. Programmed learning, computer-aided instruction and interactive video all have one thing in common: they allow the trainee to learn at his or her own pace. Also, they allow material already learned to be bypassed in favour of material with which a trainee is having difficulty. After the introductory period, the instructor need not be present, and the trainee can learn as his or her time allows. These methods sound good, but may be beyond the resources of some small businesses.

Laboratory training is conducted for groups by skilled trainers. It usually is conducted at a neutral site and is used by upper- and middle management trainees to develop a spirit of teamwork and an increased ability to deal with management and peers. It can be costly and usually is offered by larger small businesses.

Who actually conducts the training depends on the type of training needed and who will be receiving it. On-the-job training is conducted mostly by supervisors; off-the-job training, by either in-house personnel or outside instructors.

In-house training is the daily responsibility of supervisors and employees. Supervisors are ultimately responsible for the productivity and, therefore, the training of their subordinates. These supervisors should be taught the techniques of good training. They must be aware of the knowledge and skills necessary to make a productive employee. Trainers should be taught to establish goals and objectives for their training and to determine how these objectives can be used to influence the productivity of their departments. They also must be aware of how adults learn and how best to communicate with adults. Small businesses need to develop their supervisors' training capabilities by sending them to courses on training methods. The investment will pay off in increased productivity.

There are several ways to select training personnel for off-the-job training programmes. Many small businesses use in-house personnel to develop formal training programmes to be delivered to employees off line from their normal work activities, during company meetings or individually at prearranged training sessions. There are many outside training sources, including consultants, technical and vocational schools, continuing education programmes, chambers of commerce and economic development groups. Selecting an outside source for training has advantages and disadvantages. The biggest advantage is that these organisations are well versed in training techniques, which is often not the case with in-house personnel.

The disadvantage of using outside training specialists is their limited knowledge of the company's product or service and customer needs. These trainers have a more general knowledge of customer satisfaction and needs. In many cases, the outside trainer can develop this knowledge quickly by immersing himself or herself in the company prior to training the employees. Another disadvantage of using outside trainers is the relatively high cost compared to in-house training, although the higher cost may be offset by the increased effectiveness of the training. Whoever is selected to conduct the training, either outside or in-house trainers, it is important that the company's goals and values be carefully explained.

Training programme administration

Having planned the training programme properly, you must now administer the training to the selected employees. It is important to follow through to make sure the goals are being met. Questions to consider before training begins include:

— Location.

— Facilities.

— Accessibility.

— Comfort.

— Equipment.

— Timing.

Careful attention to these operational details will contribute to the success of the training programme. An effective training programme administrator should follow these steps:

— Define the organisational objectives.

— Determine the needs of the training programme.

— Define training goals.

— Develop training methods.

— Decide whom to train.

— Decide who should do the training.

— Administer the training.

— Evaluate the training programme.

Following these steps will help an administrator develop an effective training programme to ensure that the firm keeps qualified employees who are productive, happy workers. This will contribute positively to the bottom line.

Training Evaluation

Training should be evaluated several times during the process. Determine these milestones when you develop the training. Employees should be evaluated by comparing their newly acquired skills with the skills defined by the goals of the training programme. Any discrepancies should be noted and adjustments made to the training programme to enable it to meet specified goals. Many training programmes fall short of their expectations simply because the administrator failed to evaluate its progress until it was too late. Timely evaluation will prevent the training from straying from its goals.

Most Managers Don't Train Employees

Most managers recognise that continuous learning in today's marketplace is essential. They know they are in the "Information Age." They want a competitive high performance organisation but they just don't know where to begin. There are five key reasons why managers don't train their employees.

They Don't Have the Time They are so busy doing more and more with less and less that they simply don't have the time. And, of course, this can be fatal to an organisation over time. What happens to a company in today's competitive marketplace who doesn't continually invest in upgrading the skills of their employees? It's the same thing that would happen to a championship football or baseball team that doesn't practice every day. Soon, they are no longer a winner.

They Don't Know How to Do It Many managers are confronted by employees who want training. These people want to develop their skills and help their companies succeed. Their managers just don't know how to respond. So, like many people, when they don't know how to do something they will avoid it. They Don't Know What Material to Use There are literally thousands of books, and videos available to companies for training purposes. So, which ones do they choose? This is why my management, sales, and motivational materials are so valuable. We have carefully selected the materials, modularised the content so that each video is full of good ideas that can be easily applied in the workplace.

Employee Training

You can have the greatest business model in the world and the best systems, but if your people can't handle the growth, you're still toast. If your company isn't investing in training, think about all the companies you admire as models for doing business right. You'll not only find that they've got a good training programme, but training is a part of their culture. If you ask them why they train, they probably would look at you like you were from Mars, because it's like asking them why they breathe. If you want to breathe some life into your operation, start by investing in your people: train them.

Employee Recruitment

Employee recruitment in the workplace is essential to a companies long term success. By hiring correctly, your organisation adds the talent it needs and can enjoy the benefits in increased productivity and morale. However this process is not simple and if the careful process of selection is not followed ; you can be mired with poorly skilled, unmotivated and unloyal labourforce with can impact future profits as well as other employee behaviour.

Recruitment Agencies

Recruitment agencies can bridge the gap between businesses and prospective employees. While hiring internally can be possible for many employees it can be seen as a waste of time, resources and money. Through hiring externally the process of selection has been dealt with by the recruitment agencies. There careful selection of candidates through resume analysis, interviews, manual and computer tests take the hard process out of choosing the right employee. Is it worth the cost to pay recruitment agencies ? In many ways companies do save on recruiting externally. Do not have to pay to advertise for the position Do not waste labour reviewing and interviewing Have professionals who understand the needs of the employers and are specialised in recruiting the right personnel.

Employee Retention and Motivation

Everyone knows that retaining top talent is essential to organisational success. How to succeed in Employee Retention To maintain a stable workforce, employers must deliberately engage in retention activities. These efforts range from re-recruiting interviews to family activities and individualised compensation packages. People need to feel wanted, valued, appreciated. They want to do meaningful work and have some say in how their jobs are designed, managed, and measured. Today's employees want to be stable, but are often "chased out" by those who are more concerned with power and position than with caring for people.

Looking beyond Retention

Clearly a competitive advantage in today's turbulent employment environment is not achieved easily. Building a stable workforce takes considerably more than just throwing money at people or giving them use of a fancy car. There's more involved than just a lot of aggressive recruiting or strong attention to retention. To achieve workforce stability, with all its financial and operational advantages, employers must invest energy in resources in a range of discrete strategies. When woven together, these various aspects create a comprehensive model for building and maintaining that coveted condition of a solid, stable workforce that drives more dollars to the bottom line.

Employee Training Specialists

Employee training specialists plan and organise instructional activities. The first day on the job makes nearly everyone nervous. This is especially true for your first "real" job. You depend on the money you make to live, and you want to do a good job. Thankfully, most companies offer training before you officially start your job duties. Some companies have employee training specialists, people who make sure you learn new skills and understand your job so that you can succeed. And, if things change say, you switch to a new kind of computer they can help you learn the new system as well.

Employee training specialists conduct orientation sessions for new employees. They also arrange on-the-job training for employees. For new employees, they organise courses that will teach them the skills they need for their jobs. For current employees, they set up courses to help them maintain their skills. They also set up courses to prepare workers for jobs that require more skill, such as a management position or even an executive job.

Programme development is an important part of the job for training specialists. They identify and assess training needs in their firms or for companies they contract with. They do this by talking to managers and supervisors. Specialists also periodically evaluate training programmes. They assess the training materials developed by course instructors. In addition, they assess the quality of the teaching done by instructors. Specialists send instructors who do not meet their standards to courses to improve their teaching skills.

Because training specialists organise and supervise training programmes, they have many administrative tasks. They hire instructors and assign them to courses. They make sure instructors have all the materials they need to lead their courses. This includes lecture materials, handouts, and other visual aids. They also develop activities to help trainees and employees learn, such as group exercises, role-playing, and discussions. In addition, they schedule when and where classes will be taught. To help instructors be consistent in their teaching procedures, specialists develop manuals and guides for them to follow. Many employee training specialists also teach classes and conduct training themselves.

Another major administrative task is to monitor the effectiveness of the training programmes. Thus, specialists maintain records about which training courses employees take. They write reports about the effects of training on employees. They also monitor the cost of training. Specialists make sure they stay within their budget, and write reports about where they spend their money. They may present these reports to their supervisors or talk to them about training programmes. New training techniques are constantly being developed. Thus, training specialists must keep their knowledge of these techniques up-to-date. They attend meetings and seminars to learn about new ideas. They also read magazines and journals.

New Employee Orientation

Effectively orienting new employees to the campus and to their positions is critical to establishing successful, productive working relationships. The employee's first interactions with you should create a positive impression of your department and the campus. The time you spend planning for the new person's first days and weeks on the job will greatly increase the chance for a successful start.

Guiding Principles

An effective orientation will:

- Foster an understanding of the campus culture, its values, and its diversity
- Help the new employee make a successful adjustment to the new job
- Help the new employee understand her role and how she fits into the total organisation
- Help the new employee achieve objectives and shorten the learning curve
- Help the new employee develop a positive working relationship by building a foundation of knowledge about campus mission, objectives, policies, organisation structure, and functions

The new employee orientation process begins before the employee comes to work. Planning ahead for your new employee's arrival will allow you to spend productive time on that first day. So, before the employee arrives you should:

- Notify everyone in your unit that a new person is starting and what the person's job will be. Ask the other staff members to welcome the new employee and encourage their support.
- Prepare interesting tasks for the employee's first day.
- Make a copy of the job description card, Brassring job vacancy listing (JVL), job performance standards, campus organisation chart, and your department's organisation chart.

— Enroll the employee in the New Employee Welcome & Orientation class through the Employee Development & Training Unit in Human Resources. Ensure that they are enrolled in the Benefits Orientation as well. Enrolment in the on-line or classroom versions can be accomplished at:

— Make sure the employee's work location is available, clean, and organised.

— Make sure a copy of the appropriate personnel policy manual or contract is available for the employee.

— Have a benefits information package available.

— If possible, identify a staff member to act as a buddy for the first week.

— Put together a list of key people the employee should meet and interview to get a broader understanding of their roles

— Arrange for a building pass, parking pass, and IDs if necessary.

— Draft a training plan for the new employee's first few months.

A new employee may be anxious about starting a new job. Try to create a comfortable environment and remember not to overwhelm the new employee with too much information on the first day. Orientation is a continuing process, so there will be plenty of time to give the employee all the necessary information. On the first day, you should:

— Give a warm welcome and try to reduce any nervousness the new employee may feel.

— Discuss your plan for first day.

— Introduce the employee to other staff members.

— Arrange to have lunch with the new employee.

— Show the new employee around the office.

— Review the job description card and organisational charts with the employee.

— Explain ridesharing and transportation services.

— Review telephone, fax, e-mail, and Internet use

— Give the employee the New Employee Benefits Packet. Be sure to discuss any questions or refer the employee to your Department Benefits Counsellor. Remind the employee to fill out and submit benefits forms on time.

— Explain that hotel policy and collective bargaining agreements call for most new employees to complete a probationary period before they become regular status employees. Discuss what the probationary period is all about and explain how and when the employee's performance will be appraised during the probationary period.

— Have the new employee complete all the necessary personnel forms.

Over the next few weeks, schedule meetings with the employee to discuss the following:

— Employee's overall impressions. Find out how the employee perceives your department so far. If there are any problems or concerns, address them.

— Organisation of the Hotel. Spend time explaining the Hotel's structure. Talk about where your department fits in and how it relates to other departments on campus.

— Mission statements. Discuss the mission statement of the Hotel and how the goals and objectives of your department help support that mission.

— Performance evaluation process. Explain that you and the new employee will be developing a performance plan, discussing her progress and evaluating her performance. Explain the timing of appraisals and the methods you'll use to measure progress.

— Department work rules. Review your department's work rules with the new employee. Discuss attendance guidelines, call-in procedures, and requests for time off.

— Controlled substances. Explain that the Hotel does not tolerate the use of illegal substances or abuse of legal substances on the premises or reporting to work in an unsafe condition. You are required by law to give the new employee a copy of the campus Substance Abuse Packet.

— Security. Discuss your department guidelines on security, such as keeping doors, cabinets, and file drawers locked, and wearing the id badge.

— Safety. Review the Hotel's policies and your department's policies on safety in the workplace with your new employee. Evacuation procedures, emergency preparedness guidelines.

— Injuries on the job. Discuss procedures for handling injuries on the job. Tell the employee to report all job-related injuries to you, regardless of how minor.

— Training plan. Discuss your training plan with the employee. Consider incorporating any changes the employee suggests. Implement any changes that you both agree upon.

— Other resources. Tell the employee about any other resources that will help get the job done, Accounting, your department's Personnel Manager, or Mail Services.

— Employee Services. Describe the roles of the

Ombudsperson, CARE Services, Wellness Programme, and the Campus Personnel Office.

Performance Management

Setting and clearly communicating performance standards and expectations, observing and providing feedback, and conducting appraisals enables you to achieve the best results through managing employee performance. To begin the process, you and the employee will collaborate on the development of performance standards. You will develop a performance plan that directs the employee's efforts toward achieving specific results, to support organisational growth as well as the employee's professional growth. Discuss goals and objectives throughout the year, providing a framework to ensure employees achieve results through coaching and mutual feedback. At the end of the rating period, you will appraise the employee's performance against existing standards, and establish new goals together for the next rating period. As the immediate supervisor, you play an important role; your closest interaction with the employee occurs at this level.

Observation and Feedback

Once performance objectives and standards are established and clearly communicated, you should observe employees' performance and provide feedback. You have a responsibility to recognise and reinforce strong performance by an employee, and identify and encourage improvement where it is needed. You provide informal feedback almost every day. By observing and providing detailed feedback, you play a critical role in the employee's continued success and motivation to meet your performance expectations.

Coaching is a method of strengthening communication between you and the employee. It helps to shape performance and increase the likelihood that the employee's results will meet your expectations. Coaching sessions provide you and the employee the opportunity to discuss progress toward meeting mutually-established standards and goals. A coaching session focuses on one or two aspects of performance, rather than the total review that takes place in a performance evaluation.

Guiding Principles

Effective coaching can:

— Strengthen communication between you and the employee

— Help the employee attain performance objectives

— Increase employee motivation and commitment

— Maintain and increase the employee's self-esteem

— Provide support

Elements of Coaching

To make your coaching session effective, you must understand the key elements of coaching:

— Coach when you want to focus attention on any specific aspect of the employee's performance.

— Observe the employee's work and solicit feedback from others.

— When performance is successful, take the time to understand why.

— Advise the employee ahead of time on issues to be discussed.

— Discuss alternative solutions.
— Agree on action to be taken.
— Schedule follow-up meeting(s) to measure results.
— Recognise successes and improvements.
— Document key elements of coaching session.

Coaching provide effective feedback you must understand the elements of performance and analyse marginal performance. Keep these questions in mind:

— How is the employee expected to perform?
— Does the employee understand these expectations? If not, why not?
— Does the employee know what successful results look like? How do you know?
— Does the employee know the performance is marginal? How do you know?
— Are there obstacles beyond the employee's control? Can you remove them?
— Has the employee ever performed this task satisfactorily?
— Is the employee willing and able to learn?
— Does satisfactory performance result in excessive work being assigned?
— Does unsatisfactory performance result in positive consequences such as an undesirable task being reassigned?

Coaching Behaviours

To make the most of coaching the employee, remember to practice these coaching behaviours:

— Focus on behaviour, not personality.
— Ask the employee for help in problem identification

and resolution. Use active listening to show you understand.

— Set specific goals and maintain communication.

— Use reinforcement techniques to shape behaviour.

If you conduct a coaching session to provide positive feedback to the employee, keep the following ideas in mind:

— Describe the positive performance result or work habit using specific details.

— Solicit your employee's opinion of the same product or behaviour.

— Ask the employee to identify elements that contributed to success (adequate time or resources, support from management or other employees, the employee's talent and interest in the project).

— Discuss ways in which you and the employee can support continued positive results.

— Reinforce for the employee the value of the work and how it fits in with the mission, vision, values and goals of the work unit or department.

— Show your appreciation of the positive results and your confidence that the employee will continue to perform satisfactorily.

— Document your discussion for the employee's file, as you would all coaching and counselling sessions, noting day, date, time and key elements.

When you conduct a coaching session to improve performance, you may want to use the following format:

— Describe the issue or problem, referring to specific behaviours.

— Involve the employee in the problem-solving process.

— Discuss causes of the problem.

— Identify and write down possible solutions.

— Decide on specific actions to be taken by each of you.

— Agree on a follow-up date.

— Document key elements of the session.

If your coaching session is conducted to address poor work habits such as continued tardiness, keep these steps in mind:

— Describe in detail the poor work habit observed.

— Say why it concerns you. Tie it to the performance standards and goals.

— Ask why it occurred and listen nonjudgmentally to the explanation. Describe the need for change and ask for ideas.

— Discuss each idea and offer your help.

— Agree on specific actions to be taken and set a specific follow-up date.

— Document results from the session.

Other Resources

The Performance Management Programme Relevant personnel policies and collective bargaining agreements UCSF Supervisory Certification Programme including "Setting Performance Expectations", and "Coaching for Performance".

PERFORMANCE APPRAISAL

The campus carries out its mission through the individual and collective contributions of its employees. To do their best, staff members need to know that those contributions will be recognised and acknowledged. Overseeing performance and providing feedback is not an isolated event, but rather an ongoing process that takes place throughout the year.

The performance appraisal is part of that process, and provides an excellent opportunity for you to communicate with the employee about past performance, evaluate the employee's job satisfaction, and make plans for the employee's future performance. Remember that the performance appraisal summarizes the employee's contributions over the entire appraisal period (usually one year). It is not a step in the disciplinary process. It may occur as often as you believe is necessary to acknowledge the employee for accomplishments and to plan together for improved performance.

Guiding Principles

The goal of the performance appraisal process is to help the employee feel:

— Positive about the job

— Motivated to do well and to develop

— Benefited by specific, constructive feedback

— Appreciated for specific contributions

— Informed about current and future performance objectives

— Involved as a participant in the process

Performance Appraisal Process

Both you and the employee play an important role in creating a productive performance appraisal process. Here are some suggestions to get the employee involved:

— Schedule a mutually convenient time and place for the performance appraisal discussion. Allow enough time and ensure privacy.

— Explain that you would like the discussion to be a dialogue, with input from both of you included in the final written document.

— Give the employee some options about how to prepare for the discussion. For example:

— Ask the employee to prepare a self-evaluation using the same form you will use for your draft. The employee can address accomplishments and things that could be done better. Explain that you will be doing the same and that you may exchange these documents a few hours before your meeting

— Give the employee a list of questions to consider to evaluate his own performance. Sample questions might be:

— What have been your major accomplishments?

— What could you have done better?

— What could I do as your supervisor to help you do your job better?

— Would you like to see your responsibilities change? If so, how?

— Prepare a draft appraisal, making sure you have as much information as possible, including:

— job description

— performance standards

— previous appraisals

— letters of commendation and/or criticism

— samples of work

— records of disciplinary action

— Consider the question, What can I do to help the employee do the job better and achieve developmental goals?

Appraisal Discussion

Continue the momentum you have established throughout the year with your ongoing dialogue about performance. You want to set the tone for an open and productive discussion. Here are some steps you can take to make it as successful as possible:

— Create a supportive environment by stating clearly the purpose of the discussion. Be as non-threatening and open as possible since the employee may be tense or uncomfortable.

— Discuss key areas of responsibility and give examples of specific results. Have the employee go first, based on the self-appraisal or the questions you provided in advance. Ask lots of questions and get clarification to make sure you understand the employee's point of view.

— Discuss what could have been done better. Identify your concerns and listen to the employee's explanations.

— Ask your employee for help in resolving problems. Focus on future performance and be sure the employee takes responsibility for improvement.

— Make sure you and the employee have an understanding the same understanding of future expectations regarding performance.

— Give positive recognition for performance that reinforces the goals of the work unit.

Discuss the employee's interests and potential new responsibilities. Discuss both of your roles in achieving new objectives while maintaining ongoing responsibilities.

— Conclude on a positive note, emphasizing the benefits of your dialogue.

Final Appraisal Document

Record the results of your discussion on the performance appraisal form. Ask the employee to sign the form, and explain that this signature acknowledges discussion of the contents, not necessarily agreement with them. Route to your manager for final signatures and placement in the employee's departmental personnel file. Give a copy of the signed appraisal to the employee.

Performance Standards

Performance expectations are the basis for appraising employee performance. Written performance standards let you compare the employee's performance with mutually understood expectations and minimize ambiguity in providing feedback.

Having performance standards is not a new concept; standards exist whether or not they are discussed or put in writing. When you observe an employee's performance, you usually make a judgment about whether that performance is acceptable. How do you decide what's acceptable and what's unacceptable performance? The answer to this question is the first step in establishing written standards. Standards identify a baseline for measuring performance. From performance standards, supervisors can provide specific feedback describing the gap between expected and actual performance.

Guiding Principles

Effective performance standards:

- Serve as an objective basis for communicating about performance
- Enable the employee to differentiate between acceptable and unacceptable results

— Increase job satisfaction because employees know when tasks are performed well
— Inform new employees of your expectations about job performance
— Encourage an open and trusting relationship with employees

Write performance standards for each key area of responsibility on the employee's job description. The employee should participate actively in their development. Standards are usually established when an assignment is made, and they should be reviewed if the employee's job description is updated. The discussion of standards should include the criteria for achieving satisfactory performance and the proof of performance (methods you will use to gather information about work performance).

Characteristics of Performance Standards

Standards describe the conditions that must exist before the performance can be rated satisfactory. A performance standard should:

— Be realistic, in other words, attainable by any qualified, competent, and fully trained person who has the authority and resources to achieve the desired result
— Describe the conditions that exist when performance meets expectations
— Be expressed in terms of quantity, quality, time, cost, effect, manner of performance, or method of doing
— Be measurable, with specified method(s) of gathering performance data and measuring performance against standards

Expressing Performance Standards

The terms for expressing performance standards are outlined below:

— Quantity: specifies how much work must be completed within a certain period of time, e.g., enters 30 enrolment per day.

— Quality: describes how well the work must be accomplished. Specifies accuracy, precision, appearance, or effectiveness, e.g., 95% of documents submitted are accepted without revision.

— Timeliness: answers the questions, By when?, How soon?, or Within what period?, e.g., all work orders completed within five working days of receipt.

— Effective Use of Resources: used when performance can be assessed in terms of utilisation of resources: money saved, waste reduced, etc., e.g., the computer handbook project will be completed with only internal resources.

— Effects of Effort: addresses the ultimate effect to be obtained; expands statements of effectiveness by using phrases such as: so that, in order to, or as shown by, e.g., establish inventory levels for storeroom so that supplies are maintained 100% of the time.

— Manner of Performance: describes conditions in which an individual's personal behaviour has an effect on performance, e.g., assists other employees in the work unit in accomplishing assignments.

— Method of Performing Assignments: describes requirements; used when only the officially-prescribed policy, procedure, or rule for accomplishing the work is acceptable, e.g., 100A Forms are completed in accordance with established office procedures.

Performance Measurements

Since one of the characteristics of a performance standard is that it can be measured, you should identify how and where evidence about the employee's performance will be gathered. Specifying the performance measurements when the responsibility is assigned will help the employee keep track of his progress, as well as helping you in the future performance discussions.

There are many effective ways to monitor and verify performance, the most common of which are:

— Direct observation

— Specific work results (tangible evidence that can be reviewed without the employee being present)

— Reports and records, such as attendance, safety, inventory, financial records, etc.

— Commendations or constructive or critical comments received about the employee's work

Around the Office

In addition to the job description and the performance standards and expectations you establish for your employees, other tools help them do their jobs. These tools can consist of a desk manual, work rules and guidelines on office procedures. Job aids such as these can provide continuity and equity in the workplace when implementing policies and procedures, allow the

Desk Manuals

Desk manuals can be a great resource for employees, especially if you have several employees performing similar tasks, or if certain tasks must be performed in a specific way. Desk manuals can be developed by you and/or your employee and should be easily accessible. Set time aside for updating the manual as necessary.

The manual should include:

— Instructions on how to use the manual
— Definitions of procedures or processes
— Information about when and where to get help
— Other resources and references

Work Rules

Many rules are already in place in the form of policies, contracts, procedures, regulations, laws, and mandates. These rules determine the actions of the Hotel, departments, and employees, and actions to be taken by you as a supervisor. Work rules may be needed for direct guidance for employees, covering their day-to-day responsibilities outside specific, work-related performance standards for their position. If you are establishing new work rules or changing existing work rules, the Labour and Employee Relations Unit in Human Resources must notify the appropriate exclusive representative.

Establishing Work Rules

Work rules should be:

— Necessary. Is there a need for clearly defined, written work rules?
— Reasonable. Rules should make supervision easier.
— In compliance with existing policy, contracts, and laws.
— Beneficial to your employees as they conduct the department's business.
— Clear. There should be no question about the intent of the language.

— Enforceable. Be willing to enforce the work rules after they are established.

— Publicised. Posted on departmental bulletin boards, covered in staff meetings, distributed to each employee, and made part of an employee's orientation and information packet.

Rules of Work Rules

Follow these guidelines to make your work rules as effective as possible:

— DO. Consult with your Labour and Employee Relations Analyst so you get off on the right track.

— DO. Write rules that are practical for you to monitor.

— DO. Make sure you are willing to apply them evenly to ALL employees in the job category.

— DO. Be prepared to provide oral communications to employees who may have reading or language difficulties.

— DO. Review after contract negotiations or policy revisions to ensure rules comply with the contract or policy.

— DON'T. Repeat a law, policy, or contract.

— DON'T. Violate a law, policy, or contract.

— DON'T. Include performance standards in work rules.

— DON'T. Use wording that is vague.

DON'T. Institute verbal work rules.

— DON'T. Phase in rules after they are issued; start enforcing them on the effective date.

Sample Department Work Rules

Proper Notice for Sick Leave: Employees must call their

immediate supervisor or designated contact within thirty minutes of their beginning work time if they will be absent due to illness or other unforeseen circumstances. Exceptions to this rule will be considered on an individual basis.

Use of Department Vehicle: Employees must have a valid California driver's license, must be on department business, and should reserve the car at least one day in advance. Reservations are on a first come, first served basis. The employee is responsible for obeying traffic regulations.

Break Periods: Breaks should be taken at the work site in predesignated areas. Employees who wish to leave the work site must receive permission from their immediate supervisor or manager.

Equipment, Supplies, and other Hotel Property: No department supplies and equipment are to be taken out of the building for personal use. Abuse, misuse, or theft of supplies or equipment, or defacement or abuse of Hotel property will result in disciplinary and/or legal action

Hours of Work

A work schedule is the normal hours of work on specific days within a 40-hour work week. Work hours for employees, including salaried and hourly employees, are based on a schedule determined by your supervisor and/or manager. Scheduling work hours includes work days, starting and stopping time, lunches, and breaks. When you are establishing work hours:

— Make sure they comply with policies and contracts.
— Schedule and control them. If you make a change you should consult with the appropriate policy or contract for notice procedures.

— Authorise overtime and keep accurate records. Process payment of overtime promptly.

— Alternate work schedule may be considered based on operational needs. Check the applicable labour contract/policy and contact your Labour and Employee Relations Analyst for further information.

Flexible Work Arrangements

A variety of flexible work arrangements are permitted under personnel policies and collective bargaining agreements. Many departments have successfully incorporated variations on the traditional 8:00 to 5:00 with lunch from noon to 1:00 schedule.

Alternative possibilities are wide-ranging, and include:

— Fixed full-time schedules, such as arriving at 7:30 a.m. and leaving at 4:00 p.m., with a half-hour for lunch

— Flexible schedules centering on a fixed core, such as varying arrival time between 7:00 a.m. and 9:00 a.m. and departure time between 4:00 p.m. and 6:00 p.m.

— Compressed work weeks of fewer than five days, such as working four 10-hour days

— Part-time work

— Job shares (a form of part-time work)

— Telecommuting, in which the employee works at home or at an alternate work site part of each week and communicates by phone or by other electronic means.

Attendance

Employees are expected to be at work on time; they are also responsible for notifying their supervisors when they will be absent because they are ill or for any other unexpected reasons. An unacceptable number of absences or tardiness may result in disciplinary action up to and including dismissal. Following are some guidelines for attendance:

— Keep accurate and current records.
— Let your employees know what is expected of them in regard to attendance and punctuality.
— Review your employees' attendance records. This will give you a chance for corrective counselling or to commend employees who have outstanding attendance records.
— Ensure that vacation leave, compensatory time off, and alternate holidays off are scheduled and taken at the convenience of the department.
— Review requests for time off for personal reasons in advance when possible. When deciding whether to grant the request, consider the operating needs of your unit and the reason for the request.

Disciplinary Action

All employees are expected to meet performance standards and behave appropriately in the workplace. Disciplinary or corrective action is a process of communicating with the employee to improve unacceptable behaviour or performance. You may take disciplinary action when other methods such as coaching and performance appraisal have not been successful.

In cases of serious misconduct, you may choose to proceed straight to disciplinary action. Reviewing the Seven Tests of Just Cause before taking disciplinary action will help you determine whether discipline is the best approach to problem-solving in a particular situation. It is prudent to consult your Labour & Employee Relations (L/ER) Analyst before initiating disciplinary action.

Disciplinary Alternatives

When deciding what disciplinary action to take, keep in mind that discipline is supposed to be constructive. Your goal is to guide the employee to improve performance or correct inappropriate behaviour, not to punish the employee. As a general rule, your action should be just enough to get the employee's attention. However, you may have to take progressively more serious actions if there is no improvement or if repeat occurrences follow. You need not take each of these actions, but you will normally take more than one of them. Your alternatives are:

Oral Warning:

— Set a time and place to ensure privacy.
— Make notes about what you want to say in advance.
— Remember that the employee may have a right to representation.
— State clearly that you are issuing an oral warning.
— Be specific in describing the unacceptable performance or behaviour.
— Remind the employee of the acceptable standards or rules. If they are available in writing, provide them to the employee.
— State the consequences of failure to demonstrate immediate and sustained improvement: Further disciplinary action may be the result.
— Note the oral warning on your calendar and key elements of discussion.

Written Warning: If you gave an oral warning and the problem performance or behaviour persists, a written warning may be effective. You may decide to use this disciplinary action more than once, to get the employee's attention. Be careful, however, not to get stuck issuing repetitive letters of warning that fail to influence the employee's behaviour or performance. Consult with your L/ER Analyst.

— State clearly at the outset of the letter that it is a written warning, and cite the appropriate personnel policy or contract provision.

— Describe the performance problem(s) or work rule violation(s) in very specific detail and attach documents which support your conclusions.

— Outline previous steps taken to acquaint the employee with the issue (coaching sessions, performance appraisals, previous disciplinary actions) and attach copies of the documents.

— Describe the impact of the problem (safety issues, need to reassign work).

— Note the employee's explanation (as revealed during your investigation) or that the employee declined to offer one. If it was unacceptable, explain why.

— Reiterate your expectations regarding behaviour and/or performance.

— Note that if the employee doesn't demonstrate immediate and sustained improvement, the consequence will be further disciplinary action, up to and including dismissal.

— Refer the employee to the appropriate policy or contract provision for appeal rights.

— Deliver the warning letter to the employee and place it in the employee's departmental personnel file using appropriate delivery procedures such as "Proof of Service."

Suspension without Pay: This is normally the next stage in progressive discipline after written warning(s) Suspension typically prevents work for a number of working days, as specified in the letter, and pay is docked accordingly. Length of a suspension without pay will be influenced by policy or contract requirements. The letter states that it is a suspension without pay, the appropriate policy or contract provision, and the number of days the employee will be suspended. It also (as with a letter of warning) describes the problem, previous corrective measures, impact of the problem, your expectations, consequences of failure to improve, and the employee's appeal rights.

Depending upon the personnel programme the employee belongs to, you may be required to issue a letter of intent to suspend, which provides the employee with the right to appeal your intended action to the next higher management level before the action is implemented. Consult your L/ER Analyst as well as the policy or contract for more information.

Reduction of Pay within a Class: This alternative is normally used when you do not wish to remove the employee from the work site, but serious discipline is appropriate. It is most appropriately used in lieu of suspension without pay, in cases of chronic absenteeism or tardiness.

The reduction of pay is for a specific period of time, related to the seriousness of the performance discrepancy or work rule violation, and noted in the letter. The disciplinary letter will incorporate the same elements included in a suspension letter. You may have to issue a letter of intent similar to that used in cases of suspension. Consult your L/ER Analyst on the procedure. ***Demotion***

to a Lower Classification: This action involves movement of an employee to a lower level position, and may be temporary or permanent.

Demotion is most often appropriate in cases of inadequate performance of responsibilities at a particular level, rather than violation of work rules. It should be based upon a reasonable expectation that the employee will perform successfully in the lower classified position. For example, did the employee previously hold a similar position, and did they perform satisfactorily?

Your notice letter and process are quite similar to those used for a suspension without pay, or a reduction of pay within class. Contact your L/ER Analyst if you are considering this disciplinary alternative.

Dismissal: This alternative is normally selected after performance counselling and progressive discipline have failed to get the employee's attention to the problem. In extreme cases, such as job abandonment, theft, or an act that endangers others, the offence may be so grave that we forgo progressive discipline.

The disciplinary actions most commonly employed on the campus are written warnings and suspensions without pay. The concept of progressive discipline does not require that you use all the actions described above, but you will usually be expected to use more than one type in your attempt to correct the employee's performance or behavioural problems, because discipline should normally be progressive.

As a supervisor, it is perfectly natural for you to feel frustrated when an employee repeatedly fails to perform satisfactorily or follow the rules. Keep in mind, however, that most employees come to work wanting to do a good job. Some will require more specific and frequent feedback than others to understand what that means in your work site and in the jobs under your supervision. Frequency of feedback will largely depend on what you observe in the employee's behaviour and performance and on the cycles of the work.

Remember that the purpose of disciplinary action is to turn performance around by continuing to identify problems, causes, and solutions. If you can accomplish it in a positive and constructive way, you will send a message that you are out not to punish, but to help the employee become a fully productive member of your work unit.

Guiding Principles

In carrying out disciplinary action be sure to:

— Maintain a professional manner by keeping the disciplinary process confidential between you and the employee

— Make a careful diagnosis of the problem to determine whether disciplinary action is appropriate

— Provide specific examples of performance discrepancies or work rule violations so the employee fully understands what needs correction

— Allow the employee ample opportunity to explain so that you have all the facts

— Make sure discipline is the appropriate tool. Would coaching or performance appraisal be sufficient to get the employee's attention?

— When you take disciplinary action, make sure the punishment fits the crime

— Help the employee improve performance by providing specific recommendations and requirements

— Communicate clearly so the employee understands the consequences if performance or conduct does not improve

Probationary Period

The probationary period should be used to ensure that the applicant selected is qualified to perform the job and achieve regular status. During this period, you should carefully evaluate the employee's performance and general suitability for Hotel employment. To make this decision, you will develop and communicate performance standards and objectives, set aside time to observe the employee, provide feedback, and evaluate the employee.

Guiding Principles

The probationary period can:

— Help the employee achieve training goals and performance objectives

— Ensure that the employee has all the tools to perform the job successfully

— Help the employee develop the skills needed to perform the job

— Confirm that the best qualified person was chosen for the position

— Foster a mutual understanding of expectations, standards of performance, and the evaluation process

— Help the employee achieve regular status

During Probation

During the probationary period the new employee needs as much support as possible. This is a very crucial time for you and the employee, so set aside plenty of time to:

— Provide the employee with a clear job description.

— Provide clear performance standards so the employee

understands what is expected and how they will be measured.

— Acquaint the employee with office procedures and practices.
— Schedule the employee for the New Employee Orientation through the Development and Training Unit in HR.
— Provide a good systematic departmental orientation for the new employee.
— Explain how and when the employee will be evaluated.
— Provide follow-up sessions as often as necessary so the employee can adjust to their new working environment.
— Provide a desk manual (if available).
— Tell the employee in advance when their probationary period will be over and explain what it means to become a regular status employee.
— Evaluate the employee's performance in accordance with applicable policies, procedures, and contracts.
— Show a continuing interest in the new employee (it's not enough to explain terms and conditions of employment and leave the employee to make it from there alone).

Extending the Probationary Period

Under extraordinary circumstances, the employee's probationary period may be extended. Extensions can be the result of a significant change in responsibilities or supervision without benefit of adequate time to assess the incumbent. There are usually notice requirements before the period would normally end. Consult the appropriate contract or policy for implementation.

Unsatisfactory performers and unsuitable employees should be released during the probationary period without delay. Delaying a release action does little to help the campus or the employee.

Questions to ask yourself before you release an employee during the probationary period

— Has the employee attended the New Employee orientation programme?
— Has the employee received an orientation to the unit and department?
— Has the employee received clear performance standards?
— Has the employee had sufficient time to understand the job duties and demonstrate performance level?
— Has the less-than-satisfactory progress been discussed with the employee? Has it been documented in a performance appraisal?
— Has the employee had sufficient time to correct the deficiency? In the case of poor work habits, did the employee know that the behaviour was totally unsatisfactory?

4

Empolyee Assistance Programmes

The characteristics of societal transitions and the process of change in general have been studied and written about extensively. The changes in perspective and accompanying transitions now affecting large portions of global society have been underway for some time. Numerous journals, books, and forums have focused on this process. The consensus among those who deal with such issues is that substantial adjustment has dominated the last 70 to 75 years. Peter Drucker, in his 1989 book The New Realities, suggests that somewhere between 1965 and 1973 we moved away from the fundamental beliefs and social attitudes that have anchored us for the last century or two.

One of those beliefs, Drucker claims, was that society was a saviour, and that good social policies and programmes would lead, if not to Eden, then at least to a vastly improved world. He contends that this belief has been replaced by a new mindset in which people question whether societal efforts can even function in a leadership role for establishing new directions, let alone accomplish "the greater good." While we may not be fully aware of the new paradigms that will emerge to guide us, increasingly disillusioned with society's ability to manage change effectively.

Interestingly, a large portion of the transition and change in which we are all engaged has occurred since World War II. The last decade, by itself, has produced astounding surprises (the dissolution of the Soviet Union and subsequent collapse of Communism in Eastern Europe, for example) which indicate substantial shifts all across the globe. The emergence of the global economy and the increasing impact of technology have also fostered profound change.

As soon as change begins, transition, by definition, begins as well. This process seems comprised of three components: endings, a neutral zone, and new beginnings. As a society, we have been in the endings phase—the dissolving of the familiar—for quite some time. Endings are accompanied by a series of predictable characteristics. These include a sense of impermanence that leads to disengagement, a disidentification with what is happening around us, a disenchantment with what we have known, and a disorientation in the more global setting.

In the United States, too, the awareness of change has intensified as the nation's two hundred year-old wellspring of good fortune has begun to show signs of drying out. Perhaps the most dramatic change we have experienced lies in the shift in our economic position on the world stage. For the first time in half a century, our country must now compete for dominance of the economic landscape. While the United States remains a major force, other competent industrialised nations have emerged to challenge it. The shifting ethnic composition of our citizenry has also caused significant change. Our population now reflects a degree of diversity never before anticipated. Emergence of the changing economic and demographic face of our society has alerted us, at last, that we are not particularly well equipped to manage the adjustments necessary for the continuing success.

These more macro changes have, of course, impacted the world of employee assistance. Establishment of the original employee assistance efforts was undoubtedly prompted, at least in part, by the stress resulting from both the pace of societal change and the changes themselves. The expansion of programme parameters beyond their initial scope has also been dictated by some of the emerging features of the new world.

As mentioned, employee assistance efforts began as grassroots movements influenced by the founding of Alcoholics Anonymous in 1935. These efforts have taken on professional status in the last 15-20 years. Today, a variety of practitioners, each with his or her own areas of expertise and credentials, offer a variety of services. The majority of practitioners now represent educators, psychologists, social workers, and those re-covering" from substance abuse. These professionals help people cope with the full range of personal difficulties, including individual psychological problems; marital, parental, and familial difficulties; work stress; financial and legal concerns; and substance abuse, which still comprises a significant portion of EAP caseloads. Current EAPs often serve dependents and retirees as well. The problems these people present may or may not directly impact an employee's workplace performance.

The level of support enjoyed by employee assistance endeavours has swelled in recent times. Initial undertakings, for example, had no benefits coverage to provide financial support for those attempting to solve alcohol problems, let alone all of the impairments now covered. As the advantages of rehabilitating previously impaired workers became obvious, however, businesses became more willing to commit company dollars to EAP efforts. This led to insurance coverage for people suffering from alcohol and other forms of substance abuse, as well as benefits for additional difficulties already described.

While appreciation of EAPs remains high at present, the changes that have taken place in the business world have given rise to new questions that demand attention. These questions have been stimulated, in part, by shifts that mirror some of the national and global changes already described. Primary among them are the skyrocketing costs to business of employee benefits, the emergence of managed care, legislation and regulations related to a drug-free workplace, and the shrinking pool of business dollars available to address job-related and personal problems employees might face. Employers and employees, like people everywhere, seem to have less faith that societal institutions are the best hope for resolving human difficulties. Since business, corporations, and the EAPs which serve them all represent social institutions, it is hardly surprising that the concept of assigning them the level of responsibility they have traditionally shouldered for solving "people problems" is now under review.

Turning to specifics, the dramatic rise in medical and benefits costs in this country has caused companies to question whether they can still afford to allocate their dwindling resources to cover the range and types of problems EAPs now typically handle. The increase in substance abuse across the United States has made the provision of treatment to those in need more costly. With its component of relapse as part of the disease process, substance abuse has come under particular scrutiny since a relatively small number of people generally consume most of the available benefit dollars by requiring repeated treatments.

The advent of managed care has also led to a reassessment of employee assistance efforts. Conceived to combat spiralling medical costs, managed care was charged with reducing spending while insuring that an "appropriate level of care" continued. Managed care efforts often contain components that appear to overlap with employee assistance functions. The most obvious example is utilisation review. Managed care personnel, usually nurses, are assigned the responsibility for making assessments and diagnoses, and then matching patients with the appropriate level of care and treatment provider. This has been an employee assistance job function for some time where mental health and drug and alcohol abuse are concerned. Some managed care efforts also claim to provide a full range of employee assistance services as part of their health care delivery system. Given this perceived redundancy in a time of scarce resources, businesses have, not surprisingly, begun to consider whether EAPs are necessary.

The establishment of the drug-free workplace as a standard for American industry presents a third factor stimulating review of EAPS. While articulating basic guidelines for achieving a drug-free workplace, management has often contributed neither desire nor appropriate funding to support the accomplishment of stated goals. While almost all guidance on EAPs recommends a combination of assistance and consequences, criteria that spell out recommended components of such efforts are neither uniform nor specific.

This has generally left direction of drug-free workplace efforts in the hands of individual organisations, many of which have begun with a comparatively punitive approach, instead of one that incorporates education and rehabilitation in conjunction with the more traditional disciplinary actions associated with unacceptable job performance. Increasingly, organisations realise that their economic interests are better served by rehabilitating employees instead of firing them, some enterprises remain wedded to punitive measures to the exclusion of all other options for handling mental health, drug, and alcohol abuse problems. The economic argument, for whatever reason, has not convinced them. These organisations also seem to believe that negative measures more accurately reflect the tone of the legislation or regulations that have been passed than alternatives that educate or provide assistance for managing difficulties.

Increased global competition has also impacted the status of EAPS. To compete, businesses must operate more efficiently with fewer resources than ever before. Employees, therefore, may be asked to shoulder more of the burden for assistance themselves, and will find relapses tolerated and supported to a much more limited degree. Accountability requirements will likely increase for EAPS, with funding dependent to some extent on demonstratively positive results. Programmes will need to illustrate in measurable ways that they are accomplishing the goals that guide them.

EAP professionals have exhibited many of the same characteristics common to other groups when confronted with transition and change and the questions and concerns that accompany them. While many view the challenges as new opportunities, others have resisted any alterations. These people see the changes taking place as undermining and dismantling what has been a positive and effective calling. As a consequence, they have had difficulty generating alternatives that would encourage the most productive adaptations for the changing world.

Where does this leave employee assistance efforts today? The answers to that question are myriad. Some argue that EAPS, as we now know them, should be absorbed into managed care or even national health insurance efforts, should that option emerge.

Others take a more central position, arguing that the need for EAPs is greater than ever, and that the efforts should continue more or less as they are now. Finally, others believe that EAPs should remain an integral part of the business arena, but that their role should be substantially redefined. many in this position suggest that the focus of employee assistance needs to shift from strong clinical involvement to a broader organisational outlook. Gatekeeping, education, and programme evaluation of the clinical aspects of service delivery might become primary responsibilities of employee assistance professionals with this point of view. Practitioners might also assume a broader range of human resource activities, such as crisis management, wellness programmes, and training and development as directions for EAPs to become better defined.

Historical Overview and Evolution of Employee Assistance Programmes

An appreciation of EAPs past and present helps lay a foundation for future planning. Historical study illustrates what has been effective in the employee assistance field by highlighting elements germane across circumstances and time. It also speaks to specifics of programme operation by documenting a range of programme models utilized for service delivery to date. In times of change, historical study becomes particularly useful, offering access to a wide range of possible options and reducing the possibility of repeating previous mistakes. A well-defined point of departure makes the charting of new territory easier and less intimidating.

Employee Assistance Programme Rationale

Employee assistance programmes have become a familiar facet of the American industrial landscape, but even today, there is no consensus as to what actually constitutes these efforts. Some practitioners still debate which elements give an EAP legitimacy. The research work of Paul Roman and Terry Blum, however, has yielded a core technology that comes closest to capturing the experience of long-term employee assistance professionals. Roman and Blum assert that for such programmes to reflect their history, they must:

- Provide effective liaison with supervisory management. This linkage includes:
  - Identification of problem employees through the vehicle of inadequate job performance;
  - Consultation with supervisors on how to refer to and utilise EAPS; and
  - Instruction in how to practice constructive confrontation that motivates employees to improve their job performance if they desire continued employment.
- Provide effective liaison with benefits management. This linkage includes:
  - Creating a network between employee assistance and appropriate community resources;
  - Creating a working relationship between service providers and employee assistance practitioners;
  - Fostering acceptance of the fact that the

workplace can be an appropriate setting for dealing with personal problems that might impact job performance, especially when those problems are alcohol and drug abuse;

- — Combining alcohol and drug abuse benefits with other forms of treatment; and
- — Insuring managed health care through cost containment and other gatekeeping efforts.

— Provide effective assessment and referral for a number of human problems, among which addiction problems are clearly the most important.

The Employee Assistance Programme Association also offers guidelines with regard to definition. The Association defines EAPs in their Standards as:

> a worksite-based programme designed to assist in the identification and resolution of productivity problems associated with employees impaired by personal concerns including, but not limited to: health, marital, family, financial, alcohol, drug, legal, emotional, stress, or other personal concerns which may adversely affect employee job performance".

These two resources capture mainstream current thinking within the field. Although various aspects of the definition of employee assistance remains contested, the reasons companies, governments, and other organisations have established such programmes for their workforce have become obvious. Primary rationales for these efforts fall into three major areas: humanitarian commitments, safety issues, and economic concerns. Managers in most organisations realise that employees are their most important asset. Even with the advent of computers and robotics, people still make organisations function. Workers, however, are human beings, and therefore face human problems. In these stressful times, the frequency and magnitude of human problems has, predictably, increased.

Assisting employees through their difficulties is humanitarian and moral act, and has often been cited by administrators as a justification for employee assistance efforts. Safety issues also motivate organisations to establish EAPS. A number of federal and state government regulations specify that organisations must provide a safe working environment for their personnel. Failure to address human problems may therefore subject an organisation to legal liability. This is especially true if suspicions about safety hazards have been reported, and the organisation takes no action to address the situation. Any of the wide range of human problems including depression, anxiety, stress, and certainly drug and alcohol abuse, can conceivably cause or accelerate safety-related problems. Costs for negligence in this area can be considerable in both human and financial terms.

The primary impetus for the establishment of EAPS, though, has been and remains economic. While estimated costs of human problems vary widely, no one disputes that their impact is substantial. The Health Insurance Association of America estimated the treatment costs for mental illness and drug abuse in the United States at $105 billion in 1989. Recent estimates of the economic cost of substance abuse alone range between $70 and $75 billion annually, representing annual productivity losses of $30.1 billion for United States businesses. To reduce such costs, businesses and governments have looked to dramatically expanded EAPS. Small businesses, too, have begun contracting for employee assistance services.

Evolution of Employee Assistance Programmes

There are many different EAP alternatives available in

today's market, with numerous organisations and individuals claiming programme expertise. Part of the reason for the existence of such myriad options is that employee assistance has become a profitable, market-driven business. To make intelligent choices between options, human resources (HR) managers need to understand underlying philosophies with regard to what different programmes seek to accomplish. The sophisticated businesses on the current scene often emerged out of humble origins.

As mentioned, occupational alcohol programmes (OAPs) were the earliest form of employee assistance. These efforts were founded by recovering alcoholics who, with the help of Alcoholics Anonymous (AA), had overcome drinking problems that had significantly affected their personal and working lives. By the late 1940s, a number of organisations had begun to recognise that employees with alcohol problems could be treated and subsequently returned to work. Profound changes in both work productivity and general life functioning occurred when drinking ceased.

EAPs at Eastman Kodak and du Pont in the early 1940s as well as later programmes at North American Aviation, Consolidated Edison, New England Electric, and Caterpillar, all possessed similar characteristics. They focused primarily on alcoholism and alcohol related problems, and their initial efforts remained mostly informal. The dedicated efforts of industrial or company physicians proved instrumental in gaining management acceptance and approval for these undertakings.

Employers aided the recovering individual initially by assuming the risk of returning that person to work. When such gambles proved successful, efforts began to identify employees with alcohol problems before termination due to poor job performance became necessary. Supervisors and certain union representatives assumed these new duties. These individuals received minimal training in the signs and symptoms of alcohol abuse and addiction so they could recognise such problems among their colleagues.

Between the mid-1940s and the end of the 1950s, the Labour Management Committee of the National Council on Alcoholism (NCA) worked with many companies, unions, and governmental agencies on establishing alcoholism programmes. Relentless trial and error produced major refinements in the creation of meaningful and successful efforts. These refinements resulted in the formalisation of alcoholism programmes, increasing acceptance in the business environment, and growth in jointly supported union management ventures. However, repeated applications of the original occupational alcohol/supervisory approach revealed some obvious shortcomings.

Charging first line supervisors, for example, with the responsibility for identifying and referring employees with alcohol problems left people above first line management largely undiagnosed. This pattern of referral persisted despite overwhelming evidence that alcoholism affects every occupational and professional level equally. Worse, it often created the impression among employees that these initial programmes were "witch hunts." Such an attitude obviously made constructive, cooperative efforts increasingly difficult to achieve.

In addition, supervisors tended to base diagnoses on their own knowledge of alcohol problems and drinking habits. Thus, if the supervisor had a drinking problem, he or she would not likely diagnose others with similar difficulties. Moreover, since early training sessions were typically brief, elementary, and not repeated, the tendency to return to personal biases and assumptions about drinking over time remained strong.

Finally, first line supervisors proved no match for practicing alcoholics with years of experience in manufacturing excuses for failures in responsibility. Lacking understanding of the disease process, supervisors often unintentionally aided the practicing alcoholic by covering up his or her mistakes. Because of the considerable stigma attached to alcoholism, supervisors also leaned toward postponing referral until they could completely verify the presumed problem. Most individuals referred for help, therefore, had already reached the end stages of the disease process, where the chances for recovery are more remote.

By the 1960s, a shift in focus had occurred in the workplace from the attempts to identify the symptoms of alcoholism to that of impaired job performance. Several factors eased this transition. First, problems with job performance carried less of a blemish with them than alcoholism. Second, the use of concrete behavioural descriptions (poor turnaround time, difficulty getting along with others, excessive absenteeism) allowed supervisors to avoid arguments over alcohol use and abuse, and, thus, sidestep the alcoholic's denial system. Third, most supervisors recognised the rudimentary nature of their training in diagnosing alcohol abuse, and so hesitated to act on it, but gauging job performance was something with which these same supervisors were comfortable and familiar. When asked to assume responsibility along these redefined boundaries, they accepted the task.

This shift in supervisor focus to job performance, however, uncovered one of the biggest limitations of employee assistance efforts to date: assistance only existed for alcohol problems. When employees presented other problems contributing to or impairing their job performance, management had no resource available to impact them. Out of this need, the concept of employee assistance, was born.

Contemporary employee assistance efforts have expanded well beyond the scope of the original alcohol approach. EAPs have generated widespread acceptance of the fact that many personal problems beside alcoholism affect (or potentially affect) an employee on the job, and have overcome some of the stigma attached to previous efforts by broadening the spectrum of care. Because a wider range of services exists, utilisation often takes place earlier, and problems get addressed before they reach a chronic and less manageable stage. Interestingly, this approach seems to have expanded the identification of alcohol abuse, and has exposed drug abuse as well. These difficulties often surface during treatment an employee has sought for an apparently unrelated problem.

Current employee assistance efforts still deal with substance abuse, but also typically address: individual psychological problems; marriage, family and child difficulties; work stress; and financial and legal concerns. Adding problem areas to the programme palette has generated what is commonly known as the "broad brush" or comprehensive approach to human problems. The Comprehensive Alcohol Abuse, and Alcoholism Prevention, Treatment and Rehabilitation Act of 1970 (also known as the Hughes Act) helped speed the evolution described.

The Act identified alcoholism as a physical and psychological disease, effectively decriminalising alcoholism and setting the stage for more systematic and thorough efforts to mobilise treatment resources for the employed alcoholic. A separate federal agency, the National Institute of Alcohol Abuse and Alcoholism (NIAAA), was established in 1971. The NIAAA began providing, through its occupational branch, considerable attention to the development of alcohol related programmes in both private and public organisations. In 1972, the NIAAA trained occupational programme consultants and published a position paper supporting the comprehensive approach to EAPS. The comprehensive concept had become the norm in industrial counselling by the end of the decade.

In 1974, the organisation of the Association of Labour and Management Administrators and Consultants on Alcoholism, or ALMACA, provided another major boost to the EAP movement. AL14ACA contributed to the dissemination and enhancement of EAP knowledge. Publication of a directory of EAP specialists has increased community and individual awareness of the EAP concept. Since the mid-1980s, credentialing of employee assistance professionals has fallen within the jurisdiction of the Employee Assistance Certification Commission of ALMACA/EAPA.

One of the more important events in the 1980s contributing to the rapid growth of EAPs was the increasing involvement of public treatment centers and private practitioners in EAP services. Government cutbacks had left a void in treatment through typical employee assistance programmes. Public and mental health agencies, alcohol and drug treatment centers, and private consulting firms eagerly entered the EAP field, seeing potential for future economic survival in partnership with industry. New concepts also emerged with purportedly preventative capabilities focusing on stress management and health or wellness and "addiction" problems. Innovative, controversial programmes proposed that controlling stress and encouraging healthier lifestyles among employees could reduce or prevent many problems dealt with in occupational alcoholism programmes and EAPs.

Some managed mental health care firms now offer services to employees that are often mistaken for EAPS. These arrangements typically involve a provider organisation with a staff skilled in both diagnosis/referral and counselling/treatment, and offer at least some proportion of these at low rates or even no charge. They claim more efficient and effective use of benefits dollars as a result, with an accompanying better access to treatment. Frequently marketed as EAPS, these services often include little of the core technology of actual employee assistance efforts. Though similar in appearance, their present structure does not provide full and comprehensive EAP services.

Continuum of Responsibilities

As mentioned earlier, the EAP concept can be viewed as a continuum of different models, each with a set of responsibilities. Adapting EAP responsibilities to the unique needs of a particular organisation or worksite typically produces both the greatest programme success and organisational satisfaction.

EAP responsibilities fall into two fundamental categories: clinical and organisational. Handling clinical problems facing employees requires EAP practitioners to engage in assessment, diagnosis and referral. Evaluations may apply to alcohol and/or drug abuse programmes only, or to comprehensive, full service efforts. In the latter case, clinical programmes typically deal with individual psychological problems, marital and family problems, work stress, and legal and financial concerns as well as substance abuse. An EAP professional's duties might also include short-term counselling (i.e., three to six sessions) for any of the clinical components of the programme.

Other clinical duties may involve developing a network of high quality treatment resources, monitoring service delivery, participating in treatment planning as appropriate, maintaining a support system for the employee in the workplace even after clinical placement, and remaining as a liaison between the treatment provider, the individual, and management as necessary.

Clinical contributions alone, however, do not define the uniqueness of the employee assistance concept. Organisational responsibilities have historically had at least equal importance. Changes in the workplace make this aspect of EAPs even more important today. As indicated by the core technology described, one organisational responsibility for employee assistance is to assist supervisors. Assistance can include consultations with supervisors regarding employee problems, developing strategies for handling problem individuals whether or not employee assistance formally intervenes, and supervisory training in employee assistance and other areas of human development as needed.

Effective employee assistance practitioners have also acted as expert consultants to other staff members of the organisation utilising them. They have often been asked to advise and lead in times of crisis, layoff and retirement. Management development and/or labour relations have enlisted employee assistance professionals to help reconcile organisational problems that require the application of discipline with the personal needs of employees who need attention and compassion. Qualified personnel have also been requested to provide interventions when an analysis of EAP records reveals that many referrals come from the same area in an organisation, and that the problems appear to stem from the same work-related source. Further, by maintaining accurate statistics on their programmes, professionals in the employee assistance field have sometimes foreseen emerging needs for health care, education, and/or training and development.

Employee assistance personnel also help manage health care, especially where benefits analysis, cost containment, and development of effective service for alcohol, drug abuse, and mental health are concerned. The organisational component of such programmes is at least as important as the clinical. Insuring the involvement of employee assistance providers in the organisations they serve maximises the chances for programme success. In the mid-1980s, EAP experts began debating the merits of "mega-brush" programmes. "Mega-brush" programmes refer to the combination of EAPs and worksite wellness efforts.

Where EAPs typically treat substance abuse and mental health problems already affecting job performance, wellness programmes deal with prevention and control of physiological and behavioural health risks before such risks develop into disabilities. The combination of EAPs and wellness programmes has some observers concerned about the possible dilution of EAP core technology (Roman and Blum, no date). However, employers' concerns about health care cost containment encourages consideration of all avenues of health improvement, including adoption of both wellness programmes and EAPS. If run cooperatively, wellness and employee assistance efforts have shown potential for complementing each other quite well.

Claims for the success of employee assistance have sometimes reached surprising heights. Unfortunately, much of the data in this area is not the product of rigorous research investigation. Nevertheless EAPs have succeeded, and, in fact, have had an impact on cases where traditional managerial intervention and treatment programmes have not. The reason for this is that individuals will sometimes face personal problems when their job is at stake that they would not face when confronted by family, friends, and clinical treatment providers.

According to EAPA estimates, an organisation sponsoring an EAP can expect up to a five-to-one return on investment through savings made possible by employee response to counselling and subsequent job performance improvement. As a result of their contributions to organisations, the number of EAPs has swelled dramatically. EAPs have a marked presence amongst the companies listed in the Fortune 500. As early as 1973, 25 percent of Fortune 500 companies already had an EAP. By 1979, 59 percent of the Fortune 500 companies had established EAPS, and today, estimates of programme operations in these organisations have reached 80 percent.

Influence of Government Regulations

Several federal laws have had an important influence on how organisations deal with alcoholics, drug abusers, and other impaired workers. For example, the Comprehensive Alcohol Abuse, and Alcoholism Prevention, Treatment and Rehabilitation Act of 1970 referred to earlier, directed the federal government to aid federal civilian employees (and, due to a later amendment, their families) in alcoholism prevention, treatment, and rehabilitation. Subsequently, the Vocational Rehabilitation Act, passed in 1973, prohibited employment discrimination by federal contractors or subcontractors against employable, qualified, handicapped workers. Amendments in 1977 to this Act ensured that employees with a history of alcohol and drug abuse receive the same rights as other handicapped workers.

These amendments also directed federal contractors to take affirmative action and hire individuals with a history of drug and alcohol addiction if they are qualified and able to perform their duties. As a result of these federal laws, alcoholism is now viewed as a legal disability, and the Vocational Rehabilitation Act has been reenforced, in a variety of contexts, to ensure the workplace rights of alcohol and drug abusers. In 1978, however, the Rehabilitation, Comprehensive Services, and Developmental Disabilities Amendments drastically altered laws prohibiting discrimination on account of a physical handicap, as well as redefining the term, "handicapped individual."

According to these amendments, an employee "who is an alcoholic or drug abuser whose current use of alcohol or drugs prevents such an individual from performing the duties of the job in question, by reason of such current alcohol or drug abuse" is not considered physically handicapped. Thus, in most jurisdictions, an employer may terminate an employee for alcohol abuse or drug addiction, except where a contract modifies the right to discharge employees, such as in a collective bargaining agreement. Even if the employer has the right, though, to discharge an employee, the employee has the right, in a number of states, to receive unemployment and disability benefits. Furthermore, if the disease is demonstratively job-related—due to work-stress, for example—the employer might have additional liability for damages for such a disability.

Moreover, according to the Equal Employment Opportunity Commission's (EEOC) guidelines, an employer aware of an employee's alcoholism or drug abuse must make "reasonable accommodation" to known physical and mental limitations of a qualified handicapped applicant or employee unless the employer can demonstrate that the accommodation would impose undue hardship upon the operation of the organisation. Arbitrators have interpreted this to mean that the employer has the duty to try to assist the troubled employee and to direct and encourage the employee to seek treatment. For this purpose, the employer must allow the employee to take sick leave, if necessary, for treatment, before initiating termination for continued poor job performance.

Although current United States law does not require employers to provide employee assistance services, some experts believe that most organisations could not meet the "reasonable accommodation" requirement without an EAP. Instituting EAPS, therefore, can establish a first line of defense for organisations against unreasonable accommodation laws and wrongful termination suits. Another piece of legislation with the potential for substantial impact on EAPs is the Drug Free Workplace (DFW) Act of 1988. This legislation requires the federal government, as well as its contractors and grantees, to have a drug-free workplace policy. All executive branch offices must develop drug-free workplace programmes that provide for supervisory training, employee education, an EAP, drug testing, and a written policy statement. Private sector employers have also been encouraged to adopt these types of programmes with the same components recommended in the federal arena.

In response to the DFW Act, many organisations have adopted comprehensive programmes, including drug testing. Some employee assistance professionals have expressed concern that the DFW Act might encourage the application of consequences" such as termination, without providing the opportunity, through the EAP process, for drug rehabilitation. The Act does not require organisations to establish EAPS, and only suggests making EAP services available as part of an alternative to disciplinary action.

The most recent piece of legislation impacting employee assistance programmes is The Americans With Disabilities Act, signed into law in 1990 and enacted in July 1992. The Act includes various time lines stipulating when objectives defined must be accomplished. Provisions build on the Vocational Rehabilitation Act already discussed and further prohibit discrimination in employment against those with recognised disabilities. Under this new law, employers must reasonably accommodate those who can otherwise perform stated job functions, unless, once more, the employer can demonstrate undue hardship such accommodations would cause. Additionally, the Act establishes that:

— employees can be tested for illegal drugs;
— the use and/or abuse of illegal drugs can be prohibited in the workplace;
— employers may require that employees be free from the influence of drugs in the workplace; and
— the workplace must conform to the Drug Free Workplace Act of 1988.

Objectives of EAPs

Employee assistance efforts typically assist employees with personal problems that might impact job performance. Currently, most EAPs utilise a broad brush approach to human problems. For maximum employee assistance functioning, programmes need both clinical and organisational responsibilities. The amount of additional responsibility an EAP decides to assume in a particular organisation depends on the specific needs of the organisation's workforce, as well as the organisation's structure, philosophy, and resources. Whatever role the EAP plays within a given organisation, its basic objectives, beyond its clinical role, are to retain valued employees with skills and experience and to make contributions to various aspects of the organisation, including:

- Serving as a resource to supervisors with personal problems;
- Assisting with training and development;
- Assisting with maximising employee potential;
- Maximising the use of benefit dollars while fostering cost containment;
- Assisting in promoting and maintaining a productive, efficient work environment;
- Maximising the organisation's social responsibility;
- Serving as a resource to union representatives; and
- Assuring quality of care.

Emerging Issues of Controversy

Over the last ten years, EAPs have received considerable recognition for both clinical and organisational accomplishments. Larger organisations now typically regard employee assistance as an essential component of the human resources (HR) function. EAPs (internal or external) have largely moved out of the fringe relationship with organisations that characterised their early stages of development. Most standard HR texts used in today's business programmes identify EAPs as part of the human resource (or personnel) function.

As a consequence, employee assistance professionals feel qualified and comfortable contributing to the overall HR mission, and HR managers generally appreciate what EAPs can bring to an organisation. Despite this recognition and acceptance, however, the function of employee assistance efforts still varies from setting to setting. The role EAPs should play in the present and future persists as a subject of discussion within the employee assistance profession. Some of the issues further explored include:

— The direction and evolution of EAPS;

— Staffing and certification;

— Confidentiality;

— Internal versus external service delivery;

— Relationship of EAPs to managed care; and

— Programme evaluation.

Establishment and Maintenance of Empolyee Assistance Programmes

Struggling with an ever-changing world has often forced organisations to make difficult and painful decisions. The same holds true for employee assistance programmes. While some employee assistance professionals view challenges as opportunities, others have found the process of making necessary alterations quite threatening.

Transition periods typically require people to move in directions that conflict with the past. For example, organisations have historically separated employee assistance efforts from disciplinary procedures, making the "helping arm" of the organisation and the arm that applied the consequences easily distinguishable. Today, because of legal or security issues, members of some employee assistance programmes have found that these distinctions are sometimes blurred. For example, representatives of EAPs in some settings are now asked to refer clients for drug testing and report test results. Similarly, a given EAP might, because of costs, find itself part of a structure that limits or even cuts drug and alcohol benefits. Such a circumstance runs counter to the recognition of relapse as part of the substance abuse picture. Today's EAPs find themselves shaped, defined, and even coerced by external forces which muddy traditional programme values and sometimes inhibit proper functioning. Such conflicts make establishing, selecting, and/or refining EAP models and functions difficult.

Current Programme Models

HR or personnel managers must make ongoing, crucial decisions regarding the general design of the employee assistance programme,? the services it will provide, and its organisational setting. The characteristics of the organisation involved, attitudes of supervisors and union representatives where appropriate, and available resources all influence these decisions. An organisational needs assessment that examines behavioural health problems manifested by employees and their families.

Studying the nature of job performance issues can provide a useful guide for establishing the kind of programme that will best serve all concerned. The needs assessment can be conducted through analyses of psychiatric health care utilisation data, employee and supervisor surveys, job performance records, and the organisation's existing behavioural health benefit plan. Estimating the potential costs and savings of implementing or modifying an existing EAP should also be done in advance, with the help of a benefit/cost analysis. A variety of organisations provide additional information on this subject, including the Society for Human Resource Management (SHRM—formerly the American Society for Personnel Administration), the Employee Assistance Professionals Association (EAPA), and the Employee Assistance Society of North America (EASNA).

As mentioned, several different design options exist for employee assistance service delivery. Any one of them can work, depending on an organisation's particular circumstances and concerns. However, selecting an EAP model should be a dynamic, rather than a once-and-for-all, choice. Given the level of change occurring in all aspects of contemporary life, an attitude of ongoing adjustment will likely prove productive and necessary for optimal programme functioning.

Lay Assessment and Referral Model

A lay assessment and referral model conforms most closely to original employee assistance efforts. It is typically staffed by recovering alcoholics who direct assistance toward other individuals who suffer similar afflictions. This sort of EAP usually operates internally. Personnel often have little or no formal training, although they generally have substantial experience. A portion of these individuals have obtained credentials of some kind in recent years. Referral resources in this approach may be confined to self help or alcohol treatment centers. Such programmes have limited scope and have become increasingly rare.

Centralised Limited Assessment

This approach, sometimes called a 'clearinghouse,' characteristically involves a service located off-site which assists one or many different types of organisations simultaneously. Service delivery may occur in person or via the telephone. The individuals providing service may have training as a counsellor, but can possess minimal credentials. Knowledge of, and the ability to administer a thorough evaluation of community resources are usually limited as well. The ratio of EAP staff to the size of the organisation is usually low. Not surprisingly, therefore, these programmes generally have marginal organisational involvement due to their off-site location and lack of intimate knowledge of the organisation.

Situational Counselling Model

This approach offers a wide range of options, generally utilising a comprehensive range of strategies for tackling human difficulties. Problems dealt with include, but are not limited to: individual psychological problems; marital, family, and child difficulties; substance abuse; work stress; and financial and legal concerns. Professionally trained (licensed or certified) counselors and administrators conduct assessments, refer to appropriate treatment resources, and monitor treatment to some degree. They may also offer some form of short-term counselling, usually for situational disorders or acute crises. Programmes like these also assess community resources in some depth.

If benefit plans do not overly restrict resources, the professional assessment, referral and treatment approach typically meets clinical needs. However, follow-up and programme evaluation frequently remain limited, since practitioners do not always have the research or statistical skills to fully assess effectiveness. In addition, organisational involvement and responsibility tend to get neglected in favour of meeting clients' clinical needs.

Full Service Employee Assistance Model

The full service model represents the most comprehensive employee assistance service, providing a sophisticated approach to dealing with human behavioural problems. It also offers highly developed organisational development resources. Counselors in full service EAPs are usually highly trained: they conduct assessments, make diagnoses, and refer to outside services as appropriate. The programme can be located inside or outside the organisation. As with the professional assessment, referral, and situational counselling model, the staff often provides short-term counselling. In fact, full service EAPs may offer assistance for a wider range of human difficulties, including clinical areas mentioned under the professional assessment and situational counselling model, but also potentially addressing such subjects as smoking cessation, weight control, managing adolescents, and other educational topics. Such efforts often engage in in-depth assessment of community resources, and options for treatment can extend nationwide.

Full service EAPs become extensively involved in organisational life. Besides training and education, these programmes can assist in controlling group health care costs, engaging in case management and/or negotiating for and administering health care costs for mental health, alcohol, and drug abuse problems. Full service EAPs work closely with other organisational entities, such as management development, labour relations, Equal Employment Opportunity (EEO), benefits, and health and safety areas. Tracking of programme and treatment effectiveness allows for increased accountability. These EAPs can also act as internal change agents and conduct organisational systems intervention where needed, either through internal resources or through recommendations for the purchase of external services. System interventions of this type can include conflict management, team building, and structural adjustments in the way business tasks get approached and delivered.

Individuals responsible for full service EAPs are often highly placed within the organisation, and have access to top management. As mentioned, staff for full service programmes usually possess good organisational skills and significant clinical training in addition to professional training and certification.

"Mega-Brush" Programmes

The so-called "mega-brush" programmes are the most recent option to appear on the employee assistance spectrum. These efforts combine full service EAPs and worksite wellness efforts. Proponents of the "mega-brush" approach suggest that this combination constitutes a new model of service delivery. The concept of wellness as a component of employee assistance services evolved naturally from the full service model described previously. Regardless of the origins of "mega-brush," the wellness approach offers an emphasis on prevention, reduction, and control of physiological and behavioural health risks before such risks develop into disabilities.

Conventional full service EAPs deal primarily with human problems after they have surfaced and begun affecting overall job performance. Wellness programmes target impacting factors that might produce problems before the problems become evident. Wellness efforts address risks for cancer, cardiovascular disease, accidental injuries, AIDS, and other health problems. Screenings offered to employees can examine blood pressure levels, cholesterol levels, the effects of smoking, weight, physical fitness, and stress. After identifying an individual's needs, programme staff refer that person to the appropriate resource, such as a medical treatment provider, nutrition counsellor, exercise physiologist, general physical fitness programme, physical therapist, well-baby care programme, and/or educational seminar that discusses risk factors for diseases or problems associated with the individual's personal and family physical histories.

However, wellness programmes by themselves do not constitute and can not substitute for an EAP. Where wellness programmes focus on the general employee population, EAPs deal primarily with specific employees who have serious, immediate psychological and/or health problems. The two programmes require different skills of their respective staffs. Employee assistance counselors must understand alcohol and drug use, addiction, and mental and emotional problems, while those who provide wellness programmes emphasize an understanding of physiology and health-related risk factors in general.

Where EAPs concentrate on impaired job performance in their promotional strategies, wellness programmes rely more heavily on education and prevention. EAP participation is confidential while wellness programmes are conducted in the open. Because of these differing skill requirements and approaches, some experts believe the two efforts should remain separate, supported by different personnel.

Future Directions for EAP Model Development

Given emerging trends, it seems unlikely that any of the programme models on the employee assistance continuum will remain exactly as currently constituted. Elements of each may survive, but changing times and needs will require variations in emphasis and structure. The success of employee assistance efforts may well be gauged according to how effectively personnel adjust to new requirements brought about by new realities.

Programme Service Delivery

Programme models define the structure and goals of an EAP. Service delivery addresses the process of realising services and goals. Organisations desiring to establish or currently operating an EAP must decide what kind of service delivery best meets organisational needs. options include in-house employee assistance efforts, contractual arrangements with an external EAP, or a combination of both. Sound decisions will reflect consideration of a variety of variables, including: the organisation's size, geographic distribution and dispersion of employees, labour management relations, use already made of contract services in other areas, and resources available for an EAP. Legal concerns about liability and confidentiality, financial concerns about return on investment, and projected utilisation should also be taken into account.

Internal employee assistance programmes

Internal EAP services generally provide full and comprehensive service. Staff consists of trained professionals with strong clinical backgrounds, including social workers, psychologists, and certified alcoholism counselors. Organisations with large employee populations are most likely to provide internal service.

Because external EAPs expose human resource decision-makers to extensive marketing, some managers may overlook the advantages of internally staffed efforts that external providers cannot match. Foremost amongst these is that internal practitioners have greater access to and more effectively understand the workings and culture of their organisation. Outside contractors with limited organisational contact simply cannot duplicate the amount of information available to the internal EAP provider.

Further, internal EAP services provide easy access to employees during working hours. Availability encourages utilisation. Having the programme so readily accessible, however, creates one serious problem: employees sometimes fear that such close proximity to the organisation might jeopardize confidentiality of services, and render the EAP more susceptible to management discovery and manipulation. If management becomes aware of personal problems, employees assume, they then run the risk of some form of punishment or loss of opportunity.

Externally contracted programmes

EAP services can also be obtained through contracts with external for-profit or nonprofit organisations. Besides mental health referral services, these outside "service centers" sometimes provide diagnoses and referrals to other treatment centers and training for their client populations, as well as a hotline employees can use in emergencies.

Organisations often view contract services as a quick and efficient way to establish and maintain an EAP. Managers also apparently believe that utilising outside contracting shifts EAP liability away from the organisation. The truth of this assumption remains unclear. Some contend that organisations remain just as liable for the agents they select to assist them as they are for the actions of their employees.

Combined programmes

Use of in-house services and external contractors or community resources constitutes yet another strategy for delivering an EAP service. An organisation desiring this type of effort would employ EAP personnel to deliver certain services themselves, and then contract with external vendors for other services as needed. The in-house EAP coordinator might assess employee difficulties and educate the workforce in general, but then assign placement for treatment and surveys of community resources to contractors outside the organisation. The EAP's internal component might also provide training to supervisors and union officials regarding programme utilisation, policies, and procedures. One such combined delivery programme is the UAW/GM EAP-Central Diagnostic and Referral (CDR) center system.

Consortia

Smaller businesses which cannot afford extensive employee assistance efforts independently sometimes unite, forming a consortium to secure service delivery. Under such a model, businesses contract jointly with independent EAP vendors to provide coverage at a shared cost.

Typical Elements of Employee Assistance Programmes

Certain elements have emerged as core ingredients for successful employee assistance programme operations. These include a written policy statement, top management endorsement, union involvement where possible, programme coordination, communication, trained supervisors, confidentiality, insurance coverage, and programme evaluation.

Written policy statement

The development of a policy statement should precede any EAP implementation. When clearly written and widely publicised, the statement serves as a guide to supervisors and managers regarding constructive handling of an employee's personal problems. It also prescribes ways of balancing organisational needs with the needs of the individual employee and the employee assistance programme itself. In addition, the policy should explain to employees that the EAP is a mechanism for providing confidential access to counselling and services, as well as reassuring them that using the programme will not jeopardise their current or future position with the company.

Top management endorsement

Top management endorsement is critical for insuring an

EAP's acceptance and protection. Internal and external programmes alike appear to require access to the highest levels of management for optimum success. Unfortunately, many organisations have not granted their EAPs the necessary visibility and top-level commitment. Organisational placement also has an apparent impact on the kinds of clients who utilise the programme. organisations assigning responsibility for such efforts to high level managers see more executive level clients. Those EAPs assigned to middle level managers usually wind up perceived as a resource for blue collar workers.

Union involvement

Depending on the circumstances, union support and involvement can also dramatically increase programme acceptance and efficiently. EAPA recommends the formation of an advisory committee that includes labour representatives where possible to maximise potential for success.

EAPs and labour unions share many common goals, including preserving jobs, furthering individual performance, providing assistance for troubled employees, and addressing situations that might otherwise result in formal grievance procedures. In recent times, unions have often initiated the establishment of EAPs through collective bargaining agreements with their organisation's management.

Staffing, licensing, and certification

Organisations must carefully examine professional credentials when establishing an EAP, whether internal or external, to ensure that the prospective programme's staff is trained in assessment and diagnosis, and can provide a wide range of mental health recommendations. As noted, alcohol and drug dependencies exist in virtually all workforces, but EAPs encounter many other types of human problems with employees as well. Recent trends in government indicate a shift toward requiring a mental health license for employee assistance practitioners, but many states still do not. Applying the following guidelines may prove useful in selecting staff and treatment providers. A proper EAP provider should have:

A state license where required, in a recognised mental health discipline (psychiatry, clinical psychology, clinical social work);

— Broad-based clinical experience, including alcohol and drug treatment and rehabilitation;

— A multi-disciplinary mix among staff members; and

— An effective system of peer review.

Considerable controversy has raged in the past between recovering individuals who act as counselors and mental health professionals concerning ideal qualifications for delivering employee assistance services. The success of self-help groups such as Alcoholics Anonymous and Narcotics Anonymous in assisting people who want to overcome their substance abuse difficulties initially fueled the debate. The fact that professionals in the mental health field did not generally exhibit much interest in addressing such issues before funds became available fanned the flames. Throw in the fact that narrowly defined medical treatment frequently winds up ineffective or even counterproductive, and it seems hardly surprising that many in the recovering community regard mental health practitioners through a smokescreen of suspicion and resentment.

The controversy has diminished somewhat in recent

times. Some recovering individuals still believe mental health professionals have little to offer others in need. Some mental health practitioners still believe that those with first-hand experience with substance abuse, but no license, have no place in the service delivery system. However, the majority of employee assistance professionals recognise that both groups can play important roles, while most recovering individuals understand that "having been there" alone does not qualify someone to handle the variety and complexity of demands professionals face in today's work place. Practitioners of various backgrounds now agree that at least some formal training and certification of personnel heightens the potential for any EAP's success.

In addition, organisations offering EAPs have become increasingly concerned about liability issues. They have consequently looked toward professionally licensed personnel to at least direct their delivery system. Experts continue to disagree about who should coordinate an EAP, but people with a wide range of backgrounds (psychologists, social workers, nurses, human resource administrators, AA members, or individuals with first-hand experience and/or knowledge or substance abuse and recovery) have performed this job successfully.

Attempts have been made to regulate EAP staffs and programmes. EAPA has established and developed an independent commission to administer procedures for the credentialing of EAP counselors as Certified Employee Assistance Professionals, thereby professionalising the field. A person gains EAP certification by passing an examination in six areas: work organisations, HR management, EAP policy and administration, EAP direct services, chemical dependency and addictions, and personal and psychological problems. To qualify for the examination, a person must log three years of work experience that includes a minimum of 3000 hours in employee assistance programming. The CEAP certificate remains valid for five years, after which a person may obtain re-certification by passing another exam or completing 60 hours of commission-approved training.

Both EAPA and EASNA have developed codes of ethics and also published standards defining what constitutes an acceptable, appropriate, and optimal functioning EAP. Despite these efforts, though, no effective enforcement of national standards or credentialing of EAP providers in the private sector has yet taken place.

Family communication and education

An EAP must communicate its availability and services to employees and their families, if covered, in order to function effectively. Verbal announcements, newsletters, brochures, posters, and payroll envelope stuffers can all be used to reach members of the workforce. At a minimum, employees must know about a company's EAP policy and understand what the programme can and can not do. Unfamiliarity with the policy and scope of programme efforts could keep employees from using the EAP, or at the very least lead to inappropriate and disappointing expectations. Education programmes also make employees aware of the organisation's commitment to helping those in need. Providing proper information encourages people to step forward when necessary and to seek help themselves.

Role of the supervisor

Supervisors have traditionally played a major role in the carrying out of EAP policies. The responsibility for training and educating supervisors to perform necessary functions usually rests with the employee assistance programme.

As discussed earlier, employee assistance professionals can train supervisors to identify troubled employees through deteriorating job performance, and to motivate these individuals to resolve their problems and improve performance either on their own or through the EAP. When using intervention strategies, supervisors confront employees with evidence of declining work effectiveness, providing suggestions about how to improve. Prompted by this advice, employees sometimes face difficulties, enter treatment, or utilise everyday problem-solving techniques to eliminate the trouble on their own. Research reveals that supervisor interventions often provide employees with all the incentive necessary to address the problems at hand

Today, the supervisor's role in employee assistance has become more complex than ever. Modern-day employees face more pervasive and multifaceted problems than their predecessors did during the era of occupational alcoholism programmes. As a result, supervisors must now act as professional mentors across a wide range of organisational activities and take a human interest in the people who work for them as well.

Ethics and recordkeeping

Many EAP administrators believe their programmes cannot function without an absolute commitment to confidentiality. Without the assurance of confidentiality, employees will not use an EAP. Confidentiality guidelines afford EAP professionals a measure of privacy as well. At the same time, programme administrators recognise the potential for conflict where organisational responsibilities and confidentiality issues collide. Conflicts of interest become particularly likely in organisational settings dominated by safety and security concerns, such as the defense industry, the nuclear power industry, public transportation, health care, and manufacturing.

A properly functioning EAP requires the ability to balance the employee's right to privacy with management's need to know. Therefore, the concept of confidentiality must be clearly defined in each organisational setting. Because state laws vary widely, developing confidentiality policies and procedures may require legal consultation.

In the private sector, EAP confidentiality often constitutes a more ethical than legal issue. Employee assistance professionals are bound ethically to confidentiality, whether or not a client specifically requests it. Every health and social service profession has imposed the obligation of confidentiality on its members based on the adoption of the Hippocratic Oath by physicians in the early days of medicine.

Because of the importance of confidentiality as a legal issue — especially in the not-for-profit sector—federal laws and the regulations implementing them offer guidelines for weighing the needs of employers, employees, and counselling staff. The 1970 Alcohol Abuse, Alcoholism Prevention, Treatment, and Rehabilitation Act, as amended and implemented by regulations, specifies comprehensive federal requirements. These laws apply to any EAP operated by a federal government agency or receiving federal funding, directly or indirectly [42 CFR Ch.1 paragraphs 2.12 (a) and 2.12 (b) I. While the Act does not cover EAPs operated by unions, private sector companies, or external for-profit EAPs providing services to for-profit companies, all EAPs can use these laws as signposts when formulating their own confidentiality policies.

The key provisions of these laws, with respect to confidentiality, are:

— Generally, no information about a client may be released without the client's written authorisation. Also, the information cannot exceed that which is absolutely necessary to accomplish the purpose of the inquiry;

— Upon a client's consent, the information requested may only be released if its disclosure will cause no substantial harm to the relationship between the client and the EAP or harm to the client;

— Disclosure to medical personnel without a client's consent is authorised only when necessary to meet a medical emergency or when a client is incapable of rational communication;

— Disclosure of confidential records is also permitted in the case of a specific court order. However, a subpoena alone is not sufficient to authorise disclosure.

Developing an employee assistance policy that clearly defines the degree of confidentiality promised by the programme provides organisations and EAP professionals with one method of handling the problem of potential liability. It also informs the employee of what he or she can expect, and helps safeguard the effectiveness of the operation.

Some organisations have chosen a two-tiered system of confidentiality to differentiate between supervisory and self-referrals. An employee's self-referral generally results in a level of confidentiality comparable to that found in private mental health practice. A supervisory referral may result in the confirming of a client's appointment by the employee assistance provider, as well as some generally minimal, agreed upon feedback between client and counsellor about what the counsellor discovers. Moreover, federal law permits consensual disclosure when there is a "need to know." Such disclosure must be limited, however, to specific details related to job conditions, and may not include information about the nature of the problem itself. This two tiered approach to confidentiality has been well received, in general, by employers and employees alike, as long as each group understands, in advance, the limits of confidentiality related to these circumstances.

Recordkeeping also will differ according to the needs of the EAP staff and the organisation. EAP records should be kept separately from personnel files and medical records, and all involved parties should decide at the outset to whom those files belong. Management and EAP staff should also determine how much information the programme should gather and keep on file, since access to records can be compromised, despite the best intentions. As a minimum precaution, assigning case numbers with a cross reference system to all records can prevent easy access to clients' names. Most importantly, EAP files should be stored in a locked file, safe from unauthorised inquiries.

Appropriate insurance coverage

EAPs also need proper benefit support to operate effectively. Unfortunately, most organisations do not include such support in their standard benefit plans. Worse, organisations faced with economic difficulties might well reduce in the future the benefits they do provide today.

History suggests several ways of addressing insufficient and inappropriate benefits:

— Upgrading the current insurance coverage;

— Supplementing existing coverage with specific plans for alcohol, drug abuse, and mental health services. These plans can be self-administered and self-insured by EAPs to encourage greater accountability concerning cost savings and treatment effectiveness;

— Contracting with preferred providers to specifically address employee assistance needs. Benefits, for example, can be paid under existing health plans or under self-administered, self-insured systems as mentioned; and

— Instituting managed care.

Each organisation must decide how much responsibility it will assume for the welfare of its employees with respect to the treatment of mental health, alcohol, and drug abuse problems. Unlimited access to benefits, however, is actually not in the best interests of employees or management and organisations have been curtailing such access at a rapid rate. The extent of benefit coverage should reflect the scope of problems covered by the EAP. However, as noted, economic constraints may force the reduction or elimination of options previously taken for granted.

An inability to utilise the highest quality resources for the particular problems it faces can also constrict an EAP's operations. In accordance with EAPA standards, EAPS should therefore regularly identify, foster, create, utilise, and evaluate community resources that provide the best quality care at the most reasonable cost. Such monitoring will permit delivery of prime services responsive to the individual needs of both employees and the organisation.

Programme evaluation

Like all organisational undertakings, an EAP should be required to evaluate its appropriateness, effectiveness, and efficiency. Measurable programme objectives and data collection mechanisms greatly assist in conducting meaningful evaluations.

Employee Assistance Programmes and Managed Care

Health care costs consume an estimated 13 percent of our nation's gross national product and have risen unabated since early 1970. Until recently, private employers and unions have almost exclusively borne the brunt of the escalation in prices through higher health insurance premiums or in the payment of direct claims.

The cost of health care is eroding the competitiveness of United States' industry. Germany, Britain, Japan, Canada and several other industrialised nations spend less on health care and have better health indicators. In today's changing organisational environment, two competing corporate goals present employers, unions, and providers of health care services with what appears to be an unresolvable dilemma. In order to maintain their competitive edge, organisations must reduce health care costs; at the same time, they must also continue to provide prompt and effective treatment to the workforce, particularly in the mental health and substance abuse areas. Such treatment retains its importance in the business community because it has had a demonstrably positive impact on workers' productivity. To help resolve this predicament, many employers have turned to managed care.

Contrary to the beliefs of many health care providers, most managers do not adopt managed care for cost containment reasons alone. The quality of care provided also concerns the majority of employers, who have come to understand that cost and quality are related, and that poor treatment services can lead to additional care, at added cost, to address the same problem.

Rising Costs of Health Care

The critical need for cost containment has lead directly to the emergence of managed care. In 1969, per capita expenditures for health care in the United States were $268. By 1990, expenditures had swelled to $2,567. During the same period, health expenditures as a percentage of GNP rose sharply from 6.8 percent to 12.2 percent, or from $65.7 billion to $666.2 billion.

Throughout the 1980s, the rate of increase in national health expenditures (NHE) exceeded the rate of inflation as measured by the consumer price index (CPI). Between 1987 and 1990, for example, the CPI ranged from between 3.6 to 5.4 percent, while the medical price index ranged from 6.6 to 9 percent, or almost twice the rate of inflation. The U.S. Department of Commerce estimates that NHE will reach $756.3 billion in 1991, and predicts that if trends persist, health care costs will rise 12 to 15 percent annually for the next five years.

In 1989, employers paid $145 billion in health insurance premiums for their employees. This figure should rise to $149 billion in 1992. Medical benefits now cost the average employer 13 percent of payroll, compared with less than five percent a decade ago. All of this, obviously, creates thorny problems for both companies and human resources departments, since these costs increasingly impact both company profits and competitiveness.

A basic understanding of factors underlying the cost structure of health care reveals the range of strategies used to contain health care costs. Put simply,

total costs = (unit price) x (units used).

This formula indicates that spiralling health care costs result from both increasing prices, or fees charged for health services, and increasing health care utilisation. Health costs first began to spiral after Congress enacted the Hill-Burton initiatives following World War II in the hopes of making adequate health care services and facilities available throughout the United States. The initiatives provided necessary funds for the construction of regional and community hospitals throughout the country.

Meanwhile, hospitals received payment for care until 1983 on the basis of cost reimbursement plus markup for overhead and profit. Employers, encouraged by favorable tax laws, historically shouldered the costs of insurance, providing employees with generous health benefits.

As a consequence of all of these factors, hospitals had few incentives to control costs. The continuing supply of government money stimulated the building of more hospitals, and the addition of more beds to existing hospitals, long after demand had been exceeded. As rising insurance costs overwhelmed possible tax breaks, however, employers began seeking out less expensive means of care, including more outpatient-based service. When hospitals proved unable to reduce capacity in response to shrinking demand, they had to raise the average cost per patient per day to divide their fixed costs among the finite number of patients.

Patients, meanwhile, sheltered from knowledge of the actual and prohibitive costs of health care by longstanding employer benefits plans, continued to avail themselves of expensive inpatient service. Physicians, too, found hospital-based practice convenient, remunerative and conservative from the perspective of patient safety. The insurance industry, too, compounded the problem by historically instituting co-payments for outpatient treatment, but covering full cost for hospital-based care. Blended together, these ingredients ignited, creating the current explosion in health care costs.

Service providers have been able to maintain their cost structures to date because (a) consumers lack the information or expertise to judge quality of care; and (b) insured consumers have traditionally been insulated from the costs of health care services, and, consequently, have not had to make painful choices between different potential providers or treatment strategies based on cost. Because they have not been involved in the process, consumers cannot properly ascertain the cost ramifications of competing service delivery options. EAPs, too, have been sheltered from having to consider the costs of alternative treatment modalities by all-encompassing company insurance benefits, and, consequently, they have tended, to date, to make referrals without attention to cost as well.

Increasing wages for health care workers, the high cost of medical technology, rising malpractice insurance rates, changing demographics, and a shift in consumer attitudes have contributed to escalating health care costs too. For example, the baby boom generation has now reached middle age when use of medical services usually increases and the type of health care required changes. Young people typically need acute treatment for time-limited diseases or accidents, but health care for the middle-aged and older entails long-term care for chronic diseases and functional disabilities.

In addition, the American public's expectations for what health care can accomplish have increased, along with the belief that health care should always be of the highest quality, regardless of cost. This attitude in effect restricts most metropolitan area health care providers to utilising only the most modern, technically advanced care available for fear of being sued for malpractice. Recent court decisions condemning doctors whose patients have not fully recovered, and the proliferation of the so-called "Marcus Welby" complex, which assumes that doctors can perform magical cures, further the spread of unrealistic expectations among users and purchasers of health care.

The lifestyle of many Americans now entering middle age has provided one final boost to the cost of health care. Smoking, poor nutrition, overeating, stress, over-consumption of alcohol, and drug abuse all lead to increased health care use. Approximately one-half of the heavy users of health care have illnesses that stem from lifestyle choices. Thus, a relatively small number of patients consume an inordinately high percentage of health care dollars. One study found that the 13 percent of health-care recipients classified as high-cost users devoured as many resources as the other 87 percent of the population.

Increased utilisation can be directly attributed to the incentives of a fee-for-service system and to the fact that many health care benefit plans promote overuse of services. The fee-for-services system, which has formed the foundation of most contemporary medical care, has encouraged doctors to prolong their patients' hospital stays, write more prescriptions, and provide more treatment, thereby earning more money for both the physician and the health care facility. Perversely, then, health care providers profit from their patients' illnesses rather than from their health.

Given these factors, it is little wonder that costs have now reached a crisis level, consuming more resources each year and threatening the competitiveness of the nation's economy. The concept of managed care, rooted in the idea of containing costs and bringing accountability to the health care system, can only gain in popularity under current circumstances.

Cost Considerations in Behavioural Health Care

Since the late 1980s, behavioural health care costs have risen by up to 60 percent per year. This rate is even faster than costs in other medical fields. Not surprisingly, mental health and substance abuse services have become prime targets for managed care.

Historically, behavioural health care costs had averaged only two to five percent of reimbursed insured medical care. By the mid-1980s though, they represented 10 to 20 percent. In 1989, treatment of mental illness and substance abuse cost an estimated $105 billion — 17 percent of national health expenditures that year. At that time, nearly two million Americans suffered from some form of mental disorder. According to the National Mental Health Association, 68 percent of people with diagnosable mental disorders received some ambulatory medical treatment, while 22 percent visited mental health specialists, and 10 percent consulted general family practitioners. The large majority of annual psychiatric admissions are actually readmissions.

Costs for mental health and substance abuse care get

unevenly distributed among treatment settings and users. While an estimated 65 to 80 percent of these costs are incurred in inpatient and residential treatment settings, only a small fraction (10 to 20 percent) of users of mental health care utilise such treatments. The dramatic increase in utilisation of behavioural health care services, and hospital stays in particular, is largely responsible for the increase in the cost of behavioural health care services.

Utilisation has increased in part because of increased use of drugs and alcohol, but also because mental health and substance abuse programmes no longer carry the same stigma they once did. More people, therefore, feel comfortable seeking treatment. Popular culture has demystified many forms of psychotherapy, too, and attached to the process the alluring halo of potential personal growth. Government support for community-based mental health treatment and financial support for training and educating mental health professionals have prompted the proliferation of treatment providers.

This proliferation has led to increased competition for a finite number of insured patients. In ordinary markets, an increase in supply (i.e., providers) would create a downward pressure on unit prices. For unknown reasons, health care has not always followed accepted principles of supply and demand. The major effect of the increased number of providers available today, for example, has been primarily an increase in utilisation without the decrease in costs one would expect.

5

Managing Human Resources within Extension

Human resource planning forecasts the future personnel needs of extension organisations. With the rapid changes in technology, needs of farmers, market situation, and competitive environment, planning for human resources has become an important, challenging task for extension. Human resource planning involves plans for future needs of personnel, their required skills, recruitment of employees, and development of personnel. Human resource forecasting and human resource audit are the two most important components of this type of planning.

Human resource forecasting refers to predicting an organisation's future demand for number, type, and quality of various categories of employees. The assessment of future needs has to be based on analysis of present and future policies and growth trends. The techniques of forecasting include the formal expert survey, Delphi technique, statistical analysis, budget and planning analysis, and computer models. The human resource audit gives an account of the skills, abilities, and performance of all the employees of an organisation.

Job Analysis

Job analysis traditionally was done for purposes

connected with recruitment, pay, administration, and supervision. But the increasing complexity of work has made job analysis an important instrument for developing people in organisations. Job analysis requires a systematic collection, evaluation, and organisation of information about the job. This information is collected through interviews, mailed questionnaires, observation, study of records, and similar methods.

The collected information becomes a basis for preparing job descriptions and specifications. The job description, or job profile, is a written statement which includes detailed specifications of duties to be performed, responsibilities, and working conditions and indicates what is expected of a job holder. A job specification is a profile of the human characteristics needed for the job, such as education, training, skills, experience, and physical and mental abilities.

Extension organisations in developing countries do not have clearly defined job descriptions or job specifications for extension personnel. The training and visit system of extension considerably improved the preparation of job charts, work plans, and time-bound work for different categories of extension personnel. However, the actual utility of job descriptions in extension organisations is complicated by factors such as work overload, seasonality of extension, the range of cropping systems, and distribution of extension service over a large area. Studies analysing the role of extension agents reveal that they face work-related problems such as role ambiguity and lack of job authority, expertise, and accountability. This shows that job analysis is needed to improve the performance and effectiveness of extension employees. Job analysis can more effectively contribute towards the development of extension personnel by adopting the following procedures which involve identifying key performance areas and critical attributes.

Areas for Various Categories of Extension Personnel

A job description consists of many details, but does not specify key areas which need attention. Further, it gives the details of what is expected from the current jobholder. On the other hand, key performance areas are specific and show the critical functions relevant at present and for the future to achieve the objectives. The identification of key performance areas helps in role clarity as well as in delegation of functions. This in turn aids in performance appraisal and training. Generally, four or five key areas for a job are identified. The core extension personnel of developing countries consists of village extension workers, subject-matter specialists, and supervisory staff or extension officers. Examples of key performance areas of core extension personnel are given below.

Village Extension Workers. People in this category (1) make regular and systematic visits to villages and farms to develop rapport with the clientele and to understand their problems; (2) undertake educational activities in the form of meetings, campaigns, demonstrations, field days, training sessions, and exhibitions; and (3) provide advisory services to the farmers and solve their production problems.

Subject-Matter Specialists. Their role is to (1) keep abreast of current recommendations and findings related to farm production by maintaining continuous contact with agricultural research stations; (2) provide feedback to the research system about farmers' problems which need solutions; and (3) train and backstop village extension workers on the latest farm technology and help them in solving field problems.

Supervisory Staff or Extension Officers. People holding these positions (1) plan, organise, coordinate, and implement extension programmes and activities; (2)

supervise and monitor the work of field staff, providing guidance, motivation, and evaluation of performance; and (3) coordinate the programme with inter-and intradepartmental agencies.

Critical Attributes for Extension Personnel

The key performance areas indicate the important roles and contributions of different categories of extension personnel. Once the roles are delineated, they can be analysed to indicate the attributes which can discriminate an effective from an ineffective role occupant. These critical attributes consist of qualities such as educational qualifications, skills, experience, physical characteristics, mental abilities, values, and attitudes needed for extension. The critical attributes needed for field-level and supervisory extension staff are necessary formal training in agriculture, practical skills and experience in farming, and knowledge of modern farm practices. Abilities in group dynamics, human relations, and communication are also important. Basic skills related to management and leadership are needed by extension supervisors. Values and attitudes such as faith in rural people, commitment to agricultural development, and concern for the whole community are important for all extension personnel .

The importance of assessing personal and professional attributes for selecting productive extension personnel has been reported by several researchers. Assessment is essential because an unsatisfactory educational level of extension staff is one of the most serious problems of extension in countries like Bangladesh, Botswana, Kenya, Malaysia, Sudan, and Zambia. A worldwide analysis of the status of agricultural extension reveals the low level of formal education and training of field extension agents in developing countries.

Recruitment and Training of Extension Personnel

Recruitment is important in selecting the right kind of extension personnel. Since the job of extension personnel calls for technical skills as well as commitment and willingness to educate rural people, an appropriate selection system is essential to ensure the right selection. The success of extension depends heavily upon selection of qualified and motivated personnel. Extension organisations in developing countries use two major sources of recruitment: from outside and from within.

Entry-level positions such as village extension workers and agricultural extension officers are filled by outside recruitment, using the services of government placement agencies. Other channels of recruitment are advertisements, private placement agencies, professional search firms, and educational institutions. In some countries, farmers are recruited to help extension agents. In Israel, volunteers with practical experience in farming, usually a couple, were recruited as extension workers to help the immigrants. These agents were found to be enthusiastic; they lived with the farmers, set a personal example, and were effective instruments for making desired changes.

Most of the extension departments in developing countries have the policy of promoting or recruiting within for middle-level and top-level positions. For example, in India, positions like deputy director, joint director, and additional director of extension are filled through promotion. The advantages of this policy are that it promotes loyalty and provides opportunities for existing extension staff to get high-level positions. However, its greatest disadvantage is that it prevents the lateral entry of talented extension personnel and promotes complacency because seniority ensures promotion.

Methods and Techniques for Selecting Extension Staff

The selection of extension staff starts with making the job opportunities known to all potential applicants through advertisement. The help of extension workers' training centres, rural institutions, and local government agencies may be sought to give wide publicity, as well as to inform candidates living in rural areas. This is followed by screening applicants to short-list suitable candidates and by evaluating potential candidates through various tests.

A typical selection process consists of the following steps: completed job application, initial screening, testing, indepth selection interview, physical examination, and job offer. In general, extension organisations in developing countries use a simple knowledge test and a brief interview to select extension personnel. By using the above method, it is impossible to discriminate an effective candidate from an ineffective candidate, because selecting extension personnel demands thorough, indepth testing of cognitive and noncognitive abilities.

Testing cognitive ability includes a knowledge test, a skill or ability test, and an aptitude test. A noncognitive test is a measure of behavioural dimensions which are important for field-level extension personnel, including concern for and commitment to rural people, empathy, problem-solving orientation, high motivation to influence and educate farmers, ability to work under unsupervised and difficult village conditions, patience and persistence, and team spirit.

A good example of selecting village-level extension workers on the basis of behavioural characteristics is provided by the extension project of Allahabad Agricultural Institute. In response to an advertisement for 27 posts of village guides, 700 to 800 candidates had applied. The final selection procedure consisted of five days of testing skills and attitudes in actual village situations. The test included testing attitudes towards menial tasks like cleaning a cattle shed or digging a compost pit. The candidates' responses to emergency situations were also tested by dropping them into isolated villages.

The assessment centre approach, originally used during World War II, can be used to select extension staff. In this approach, an organisation develops its internal resources for assessing new staff. The candidates to be recruited go through a number of simulation exercises, and an expert assesses their behaviour. The techniques used are a psychological test, role play, in-basket exercise, group discussion, projective test, knowledge test, and interviews.

Training and Development

The training of extension personnel contributes directly to the development of human resources within extension organisations. "Training programmes are directed towards maintaining and improving current job performance, while development programmes seek to develop skills for future jobs". Training has to start with the identification of training needs through job analysis, performance appraisal, and organisational analysis. Once the training needs of extension personnel have been identified, the next step is to organise training programmes. Methods such as games, role playing, simulation exercises, and case study can be used in extension organisations to create learning situations based on experience.

Training based on actual field experience should be emphasised. Emerging new farm technologies such as integrated pest management and improved practices in horticulture call for actual field experience. Extension agents need training not only in the technological aspects but also in human relations, problem solving, sensitivity towards disadvantaged groups, and the basic concepts of management.

Management Development Programmes

Management development programmes are meant to improve the managerial skills of senior-level extension officers and to prepare them for future roles. There is a great need for management development programmes in extension organisations because they face complex situations due to changing agricultural scenarios. Further, extension managers have to be exposed to modern management techniques and methods. Management development programmes have to be suited to the needs of top-level extension managers and should be based on needs analysis. Methods such as coaching, job rotation, training sessions, classroom instruction, and educational institute-sponsored development programmes are used to train managers. In India, a separate institute called Manage has been established to train senior extension managers in managerial skills and human relations.

Performance Appraisal

These are all vital activities. However, the ultimate measure of effective human resources within an extension organisation is the performance of extension personnel. Thus performance appraisal is important for effective human resource management. Performance appraisal is a process of evaluating employee performance in order to guide and develop the employee's potential.

In many extension organisations which are government departments, the performance appraisal is nothing more than a confidential judgement of work done and a character report used to facilitate disciplinary action or promotion. The employees do not get feedback about their performance. Extension organisations need to have an open appraisal system to provide feedback and opportunities for open discussion with employees on their performance, because they have immense potential to grow and develop. This system can create a healthy working climate and employee motivation.

The performance appraisal which aims at facilitating employee development has the following major purposes:

— to provide feedback and guidance,
— to set performance goals,
— to identify training needs, and
— to provide inputs for management of pay administration, rewards, and promotion.

The steps involved in effective performance appraisal are:

— identification of key performance areas and setting yearly objectives under each KPA,
— identification of critical attributes for effective performance,
— periodic review of performance,
— discussion of performance with employees, and
— identification of training and developmental needs.

Potential Appraisal

The potential appraisal is a future-oriented appraisal by which the potential of an employee to occupy higher positions and to assume higher responsibilities is evaluated. The potential appraisal can help the extension staff to know their strengths and weaknesses and can motivate them to further develop their skills. Thus the potential appraisal helps in planning overall career development of employees. Some of the techniques used for the appraisal are self-appraisals, peer rating, the management by objectives approach, psychological test and simulated work exercises, case analyses, and leadership exercises.

Performance Review and Counselling

An important purpose of the performance appraisal is to counsel and guide employees towards greater job effectiveness. Thus a system of performance counselling is needed in extension organisations. Performance counselling is provided by the manager to the subordinates to help them in the analysis of job performance, identification of training needs, and finding solutions to the problems which hinder job effectiveness.

Counselling is an art of communication involving two people - manager and employee. Counselling differs from training in that the former involves a dyadic relationship and establishes more mutuality and confidentiality. The success of performance counselling depends upon the employee's interest, a climate of openness and mutuality, and the counselling process. Extension managers can use directive, nondirective, and cooperative counselling.

Supervision

Two major functions of supervision are task orientation and concern for employees. Therefore, direction and organisation of activities, motivation of employees, and management of work groups are the important functions of extension supervisors.

Direction and Organisation

Extension supervisors have to plan the work and maintain a high standard of performance. The whole process of job analysis, identification of key performance areas, and performance appraisal will help in planning and organising extension work. The training and visit system of extension has introduced mechanisms for defining goals, planning, and scheduling work at the field level with provisions for monitoring and evaluation. Some of the management techniques used by extension organisations in overall planning and management of programmes are the programme evaluation and review technique, management by objectives, programme and performance budgeting system (PPBS), and time management techniques. These techniques have been practised by extension organisations in Asian and African countries with varying success. Personal computers offer good scope for extension managers to increase certain managerial skills.

A study of supervisory practices to improve field performance of agricultural extension in Kenya, Malawi, and the Philippines revealed the following effective supervisory practices: (1) use of collaborative, realistic, and result-oriented target setting and a daily activity plan; (2) a needs-based participatory evaluation system; (3) involvement of farmers in decision making and a reachable service target under local constraints; and (4) effective communication and use of simple proforma and report procedures.

Studies of agricultural extension in Asia and Africa show that extension supervisors must be considerate as well as task oriented, involving subordinates in decision making and treating the employees with more interpersonal competence. Up to 86 per cent of field agents in Southeast

Asia reported "friendship" as the most effective way for supervisors to ensure extension workers' reliable performance. Thus if extension managers are to be effective, they have to give supportive evaluation by way of enhancing employee motivation and improving the functioning of work groups.

Work-Group Management

Every organisation has formal and informal groups. Formal groups are established by the management, while informal groups are spontaneous and developed to satisfy mutual interest of the members. Because work groups have a considerable influence on the work situation, supervisors should be sensitive to the needs of the group and develop skills to guide and achieve the group's goal, which will benefit the organisation and the members. Effective extension supervision can use work groups in problem solving because they can provide many creative solutions. One way to improve supervisory effectiveness in extension work is to develop a leadership style which represents the extension workers' group interest at the higher level of organisation. This will increase the confidence and morale of the work group.

An understanding of group dynamics and their implications for increasing work-group performance is essential for extension supervisors. For example, in the "Hawthorne Effect," increased performance due to special treatment of the group can be effectively used in extension organisations. Studies have pointed out that well-developed group dynamics result in increased extension performance.

Management of Rewards and Incentives

An important aspect of human resource management

which needs special attention in extension organisations is the development of a reward system which will attract, retain, and motivate extension personnel, as well as provide training and promotional opportunities. Extension organisations in Asian and African countries have a poor reward system. The extension agents are not only poorly paid but are paid late and after reminders or visits to headquarters.

Most of the extension services are run by government agencies and operate under rules and regulations of public administration. These rules do not have provisions for rewarding superior performance or for a wage system based on merit. Promotion criteria are based on seniority and length of service. Thus the bureaucratic structure of extension services is a basic hindrance to designing a better reward system. Among many of the government departments, the agricultural department and extension service have a low public esteem and poor pay structure.

The rewards and incentive system can be improved in several ways. *Rewarding Superior Performance.* Extension organisations have to develop a reward system which encourages superior performance so that pay and wage administration will be an effective tool to promote performance, motivation, and satisfaction. A clear job description, performance standards, and performance appraisal will help in evaluating extension work and rewarding people for meritorious service. Ways and means have to be found within the existing framework of public administration for basing pay on performance. For example, extension workers on the basis of their performance can be sent for higher education.

Nonmonetary rewards such as recognising the good ideas of field workers or awarding honourable titles will also help in improving performance. Extension personnel may also be encouraged to form professional societies to develop and communicate high standards, as well as to recognise superior performance. A professional monthly journal or newsletter can help extension agents to communicate innovative ideas and reinforce superior performance.

Improved Working Conditions at the Field Level. The reward system must also be internally equitable. The relative importance of field-level extension functionaries has to be realised in terms of pay compensation and other amenities. Lower level extension workers often have to work under unpleasant and isolated conditions. A carefully planned system of field allowance will compensate this. The living conditions of field extension workers must be improved by providing adequate facilities for housing, transport, and medical and educational allowances for children.

Career Planning and Development for Extension Personnel. A career refers to all of the jobs that people hold during their working lives. Career planning is the process by which employees plan their career goals and paths. Career development refers to all of the technical and managerial skills employees acquire to achieve their career plans. Career advancement, which gives a picture of future opportunities in terms of promotion, is a motivating factor for performance and development of skills. Unfortunately, no career structure exists for extension personnel in many organisations.

In developing countries like India, there are many cases where one joins as a village extension worker and retires in the same position after serving thirty to thirty-five years. As part of improving the rewards and incentives system, extension organisations have to develop suitable career paths and advancement for different categories of extension personnel on a systematic basis.

As part of career development, extension personnel should be provided with opportunities to develop their technical and managerial skills to enable them to occupy higher positions. Extension personnel should have a salary structure as well as promotion opportunities comparable to other professions like health or engineering. In Kenya, the pay and career opportunities of extension workers are comparable to other government employees. Recommendations have already been made to equate the status of agricultural extension with that of agricultural research by offering an equal salary structure, professional advancement, and incentives and rewards.

Improvement of the Quality of Work Life

The earlier approach to human resource development emphasised individual development through training and proper supervision. However, with the increasing complexity of organisations and society, it was soon realised that training individuals plays only a limited role in the development of organisations. The need for improving the quality of work life through making the job more satisfying and productive has been greatly felt. Factors such as the nature of the job or the role and involvement of employees in work decisions are important for improving the quality of work life. The methods used to do so are job enrichment, job design, and role interventions. An understanding of these methods and their application in extension organisations are essential for extension managers to improve the performance of extension agents.

Job Enrichment and Job Design

Job enrichment refers to detailed analysis of the work to know the factors which make it a satisfying experience.

Job enrichment uses the job as the medium of developing employees and changing organisational practices. Some of the factors which increase job satisfaction are a sense of achievement in the job, recognition for the job, the nature of the work itself, and opportunities to learn new things and grow. The principles of job enrichment, according to Herzberg, are removing controls while retaining accountability, introducing new tasks, giving a complete unit of work, granting job freedom, and helping employees to become expert in their tasks. These principles can be practised by extension managers to increase the quality of work and job satisfaction among extension personnel.

Job enrichment programmes were successful in improving the quality of work and job satisfaction. However, it was found that job enrichment had a limited view of the job, and the need for greater emphasis on human values was realised. This led to the concept of job design, which refers to structuring a job to satisfy the technical, organisational, social, and human requirements of the person performing the work. Based on the humanisation of work, job design aims at increasing the quality of work life through treating the employees as human beings and emphasising their development and involvement in work decisions.

It emphasises the use of extrinsic and intrinsic job factors, employee participation in management, autonomy, adaptability, and variety. The concept of job design can be used by extension managers to increase participation of extension personnel in the planning and management of extension programmes, which will improve the quality of their work life.

Role Interventions

The study of roles, which are the positions employees

hold in an organisation, as defined by the expectations of significant persons and the individuals occupying the positions, is a comparatively neglected aspect of organisations. Roles are an important dimension in increasing organisational effectiveness. Through their roles, people are linked with the organisation. This linkage increases organisational effectiveness by integrating the individuals with the organisation.

Such integration increases mental well-being and personal effectiveness. The purpose of role-based intervention is to increase the mutuality of roles in organisations. Role-based interventions are done through learning situations such as process laboratory, group discussion, and use of questionnaires and schedules. Role-based interventions in extension organisations will result in increased work commitment, motivation, creativity, and team spirit.

Organisational Development

An efficient extension organisation needs to develop the capability of responding to changes in relation to its environment. Extension organisations have to cope with changes within and outside the organisation, such as changes in farm technology, communication methods, needs of farmers, rural situations, export and import of farm produce, and market economy. Organisational development allows for planned changes in the organisation's tasks, techniques, structure, and people. Attitudes, values, and practices of the organisation are changed so that it can cope with changing situations. The employees also gain greater skills to deal with new problems.

Also focussing on team building and conflict management, organisational development is a planned effort and is done with the help of an external expert in the behavioural sciences. The process consists of diagnosis of the problem, data collection, feedback of data to the organisation, introduction of specific interventions, evaluation, and follow-up. Techniques such as sensitivity training, transactional analysis, and team-building exercises are used to develop interpersonal relationships. Organisational development is an effective approach that can be used by extension organisations to bring about planned changes and to increase the interpersonal relationships among the employees.

Aspects of Recruitment Process

Many aspects of the recruitment process are now automated through our web-based HRMS eRecruit system. Much of the process takes place on line for applicants, departments, and central OHR. Applicants search and apply for jobs online and maintain an applicant profile, which they can update as needed. They can track the status of any application, and they receive email notifications at key points in the process.

Departments enter and approve their requisitions, view their applications, record the selection of applicants for interview, schedule interviews, record interview results, prepare and approve maximum offers, and record acceptance of offers on line. At the end of the process, the successful candidate's basic information is transferred automatically to the Administer Workforce part of the system so that a hire can be processed.

Staff Planning

Staff planning helps you run your department efficiently. Determining and planning your staff needs in advance, rather than waiting until a vacancy occurs, will help you achieve these results.

New Positions: All new positions must be classified before recruitment.

Replacement: If there are no significant changes in the duties or responsibilities of the position, the job does not go through the classification process before recruitment but can be submitted directly to Employment Services for listing through eRecruit.

Non-competitive Career Ladder Promotions

A department may wish to advertise a vacant non-bargaining unit and non-MSP (Management and Senior Professional) position at more than one level and fill it at the level that best fits its business needs. The range of jobs advertised in this way is called a "career ladder." To do this, a job description must be written for each level advertised, and each level of the position must be classified by the Compensation Unit.

There are two ways to use a career ladder to fill an open position:

— The department decides that filling the position at the lower level best meets its business needs. In this case, the job should be posted at the lower level and the job posting should state, "This position will be filled at the MSO I level, with potential for promotion to the MSO II level."

— The department decides it can fill the position at either level, depending on the quality of the candidates that apply. In this case, the position should be posted at the lower level (same as option 1) and the job posting should state that the position may be filled at either level. For example, using an MSO I and II career ladder, the position may be filled at either the MSO I or II level. If filled at the MSO I level, there will be the potential for promotion to the MSO II level.

— If an employee is hired into the top level of a career ladder or is hired into a non-career ladder position, the employee cannot be promoted using these criteria. Some other basis, such as reclassification, must be used.

Employees who have been laid off or medically separated from the Hotel have preferential rehire and/or recall rights to open positions on campus. These individuals are referred to as SPC (special placement consideration) candidates. Before you list a position in eRecruit be sure, you inform anyone who has recall rights to your position. A recruiter can assist you with this process.

Recruitment

Your management of the recruitment process will directly affect:

— The quality and diversity of your applicant pool

— The effectiveness of your interviews

— How quickly you get your position filled

— Your ability to choose the best qualified person for the job Guiding Principles Your goals in recruitment are to:

— Identify the talent needed to perform the job

— Attract the best qualified candidates for the position

— Promote the campus as a dynamic, diverse employer

— Meet the campus' equal employment opportunity commitment

— Support affirmative action efforts by targeting outreach to underutilised groups

Preparing for the recruitment process is essential. Before you list and advertise your position, take time to analyse the job for which you are recruiting, prepare a job description and requisition, and develop the criteria you will use to select your candidate. These are the steps you'll need to take:

Job Analysis

Your first step is to conduct a job analysis, which is the process of identifying the duties of a position and the knowledge, skills, and abilities needed to perform those duties, including:

— The approximate percentage of time the employee will spend on major duties

— A description of the major duties in order of importance

— Any licenses or certificates needed to perform the job

— The physical, environmental, and mental (PEM) demands of the position

You should also determine whether the position is "sensitive" and if so, it will require a background check.

You need to conduct a job analysis when you have a newly created position or when an existing position has been vacated and the duties have significantly changed. If your vacated position has no changes, a job analysis may not be necessary; however, you may still want to review the position to confirm that no changes have occurred.

The department may determine that it is appropriate to fill a job using a career ladder approach, which involves advertising the job at more than one level and filling it at the level that best meets the business needs of the department. In this case, a job description must be written for both levels of the position and classified by the Compensation Unit.

Job Requisition

The third step in the recruitment process is to develop your online requisition, which is used to advertise your position. The requisition should be completed and submitted on line via the eRecruit system. The information requested on the requisition is critical to the posting process; please make sure to complete every required field in the requisition.

Developing a clear, recruitment-oriented job posting that summarises the major duties and qualifications is essential to an effective recruitment process. In the eRecruit system, there are five areas where you will enter the job description information. The four required areas for your job description are designated by. Some of the important items include:

— If this is a career ladder position, that position should be posted at the lower level and the lower level job title should be used.

— *Job Title*: Select the Payroll Title for the position. You may also add a working title if it would be more informative for posting.

— *Description*: Start with an introductory statement summarising the position. In this paragraph, you will want to provide an overview of the position. You should also list the major duties of the position, using functional verbs, in descending order of importance.

— *Responsibilities*: State the responsibilities of this position by listing the expectations of the position as well as the overall duties of the job. Don't leave out any responsibilities even though you make think they are not significant. It is important that the applicants have a clear view of the overall responsibility of the job.

— *Requirements/Qualifications*: List the skills, knowledge, abilities, certificates, and licenses (including California

Driver's License) required to successfully perform the duties. For most positions, the campus cannot require a degree or number of years of experience in determining whether someone is qualified for a position. However, some positions do require a certificate or license. Indicate whether any supplemental application questions, writing samples, etc., are required. If the position is a critical position requiring bondability or a background check, this should be indicated in the required qualifications.

As required by the Americans with Disabilities Act (ADA), you should also identify the job duties that are essential functions of the position by placing an asterisk before them. A job duty is considered essential if:

— Performance of the duty is considered to be of major importance.

— A limited number of employees are available to perform the duty.

— The duty is highly specialised, requiring special expertise or abilities.

— If you have desired qualifications for your position, you should list them in the requirements text box. Be sure you designate which qualifications are desired and which are required; it is very important to distinguish between them.

— *Salary*: You will have the opportunity to enter the salary range for the position. The eRecruit system will display the salary for the position you are listing and you will have the option as to how you would like it displayed in the text box. If you prefer not to list a salary range, state that "The salary for this position is commensurate with experience."

— eRecruit also has a text box labeled "Other." In this text box you should enter additional information pertinent to this position. Anything that is important for the candidate to know that is not part of the description, responsibilities, requirements, etc., should be listed in this area. This is where you should state that a background check may be required if the position is designated as "sensitive".

— Familiarise yourself with the affirmative action placement goals identified for the position. The identified goals will automatically populate when you are creating your requisition in eRecruit.

— Determine the posting period for recruitment. Options are listed below; your recruiter can help you decide which is the best option based on the specifics of your recruitment (e.g., occupational area, time of year, etc.).

— Recruitment with firm closing date: This type of recruitment has a fixed closing date, which could be from two to four weeks or more. In order to extend the close date beyond 14 days, you will need to enter the number of days you want your requisition to be listed in the posting duration page of the requisition. The recruitment period can be extended as needed. Recruitments with firm close dates will have the SPC matching process stop at the close date.

— Open Until Filled recruitment: Normally, positions are listed with a closing date. Those that are quite difficult to fill may be initially listed as Open Until Filled, without a specific closing or review date. You will need to select Open Until Filled in the posting duration page of the requisition. Please note that for Open Until Filled requisitions, the SPC matching process continues until the position is filled.

Physical, Environmental, and Mental Demands (PEM) Form

This online form helps departments determine the physical, environmental, and mental demands of positions and recognise any accommodations required by the Americans with Disabilities Act. For all new or significantly changed positions, complete the form and be sure you keep the PEM with your recruitment file. For currently filled positions, attach a copy of the PEM form to the Job Description in the employee's personnel file. Mention any PEM demands unusual for the classification.

Submitting Job Posting Information

If there are no significant changes in the position you are recruiting for, submit the requisition. If the position is new or is an existing position with significant changes in duties since it was last filled, you also need to submit the Job Description form and the Physical, Environmental, and Mental Demands (PEM) Form for classification review by the compensation analyse. After review, Compensation will notify you of the results. You will then need to submit your requisition on line.

Targeted Recruitment

Targeted recruitment shows good faith efforts to help the campus achieve its affirmative action objectives through outreach to underutilised groups (women, ethnic minorities, people with disabilities), to ensure their representation in the applicant pool. Targeted recruitment includes advertising in publications that serve minorities, women, and people with disabilities, as well as announcements to community-based organisations and campus staff organisations.

Advertising Methods

To fill your position quickly and attract a well-qualified, diverse applicant pool, you may want to select additional advertisement. Some options you have are:

— Job Listings - Posted.

— External Advertising - Placement of ads in print media (newspapers, journals, magazines, newsletters, etc.) or electronic outlets (bulletin boards, listserves, etc.).

To request external advertising, select the advertisement options you prefer when you are creating a requisition in eRecruit. The system will require a chart string, so be sure you have it available. Employment Services will work with the contracted advertisement agency to secure an estimate for your approval, place the ad for you, and bill your department. Please note that all external advertisements must be reviewed for approval by your recruiter to ensure compliance with federally mandated programs.

Selection Criteria

The next step in the recruitment process is to develop selection criteria. These are the standards against which you will measure all candidates to determine whether they have the qualifications to perform the job. Selection criteria are developed from the skills, knowledge, and abilities identified in the job analysis and stated in the job description. To develop selection criteria, look at each of the skills, knowledge, and abilities on the job description and define the standard for successful performance of the related functions.

Example:

— Skills, Knowledge, and Abilities: Effective oral/written communication skills

— Selection Criteria: Demonstrated ability to orally convey ideas and information articulately. Demonstrated ability to read and write; ability to understand concepts and information as presented; ability to develop clear written materials.

Reviewing Your Applications

Your recruiter is available to discuss the status of your recruitment and may recommend additional recruitment options and extension of the closing date to improve the quality and/or diversity of the applicant pool. The employment assistant or recruiter will route all applications/resumes to the originator once your position has met the required two-week posting time, provided that there are no SPC candidates. The Employment office will email an Interview Data Form (IDF). This form is required to track and record all candidates that were interviewed for your open position. You will need to document and retain this form in the recruitment file for your open position.

Waivers of Recruitment

A waiver of recruitment is an exception to the recruitment policy, allowing a specific individual with unique skills to be hired without listing the position for open recruitment and advertisement. It is always preferable to list temporary positions through the eRecruit system to allow equal access and opportunities for applicants.

— *Limited Waiver.* Limited positions are those established at 50% to 100% time for less than one year or indefinite positions at less than 50% time. Departments may grant limited waivers for appointments up to 900 hours in a rolling 12-month period without Human

Resources' approval. No extensions of limited waivers will be granted. Set up systems and procedures appropriate for your department to grant and process limited waivers. Some points to remember include:

— Before granting a limited waiver, determine why the position is not being listed for regular recruitment. Check the Criteria for Waivers of Recruitment Requests to see whether the position really meets the criteria.

— On the Job Information screen within HRMS Administer Workforce, select "3-Limited" under the drop-down menu for Appointment Type.

— *Step-by-step Procedures for Limited Waivers*

Process:

— Before any written documentation is prepared, the Department Head, Department Personnel Manager (DPM), or designee should discuss the proposed limited waiver request with the supervisor.

The DPM or designee should ask:

— Why the position is not being listed for recruitment

Documentation:

— A Job Description card describing the essential duties and responsibilities of the position.

— A requisition specifying qualifications required to perform the duties of the position and qualifications required to perform the duties.

— Application or resume of the prospective candidate.

— Recommended salary offer (normally at the minimum of the salary range/grade).

Approval:

— Employment Services approves or denies the limited waiver request for any appointment longer than 900 hours.

Monitoring Process:

Departments should maintain activity reports that summarise limited waiver activities including:

— title of the position

— the name of the employee hired

— gender/ethnicity

— appointment percent

— start and ending date of the appointment

— salary

— specific unit

— *Career Waiver.* Waiving recruitment for a career position is unusual and the circumstances for considering such a waiver vary. Submit written requests electronically to Jeannine Raymond, PhD, Assistant Vice Chancellor, Human Resources, with a copy to the Campus Affirmative Action Officer, Edith Ng. The requests will be reviewed on a case-by-case basis. Please note that recruitment for career positions covered by a collective bargaining agreement is controlled by that agreement and may not be waived. Please make sure to:

— Explain your reason for requesting a waiver of regular position.

— Include a copy of the candidate's resume and job description with your request.

— If needed, request that a compensation analyst classify the position. Make sure the classification request has the proper signatures from your department and approval from compensation. This paperwork can be sent or faxed under separate cover

— *Criteria for Waiver of Recruitment Requests.* A waiver of recruitment must be based on business necessity and requires documenting the reasons that listing the vacant position would cause the department undue hardship in meetings its goals, such as disruption of critical services or research activity. Factors should include any specific constraints that would adversely affect the successful completion of a project if recruitment were conducted. Waiver requests should address applicable issues that support the need to waive recruitment, such as:

— A specific applicant possesses a unique skill, knowledge, and/or ability. Documentation should identify a specialised skill necessary to perform the duties of the position and its role in achieving project or program goals.

— Program funding transfer. Proposed hire of a Principal Investigator (PI) is bringing project funding to the Berkeley campus along with the filled position.

— Off-campus work site. Location of the job makes recruiting difficult. For example, if the job site were in southern or central California, it would be difficult to recruit for the position in the Bay Area.

— Specific skills are scarce in the labor market. Factors can include previous efforts such as the number of positions previously opened for recruitment for which recruitment difficulty existed, including the specific skill, knowledge, and ability required; when and how long the search was conducted; and results of the recruitment.

— Extreme time and/or funding constraints on project completion.

— Transfer or re-employment of an employee because of rehabilitation or medical separation (permanent or trial employment).

— I-4 separation/rehire. These are employees who do not work any hours for a three-to-four-month period and are automatically dropped from the personnel/payroll system. The appointments are normally on an on-call or as-needed basis.

— Conversion to career. Temporary employees who are assigned through employment services may be eligible for conversion to career appointments. Career conversion must be authorised through the hiring department and must be funded through the hiring department's budget. All conversions are governed by either personnel policy or union contract, depending upon the title classification. Please consult your recruiter regarding the conversion of any temporary employee to a career position.

Special Placement Consideration (SPC)

Whenever possible, the campus helps employees who have been laid off, reviewed for medical separation, or medically separated to locate and acquire alternative positions. The purpose of preferential referral is to give these employees first consideration for career positions for which they are qualified and for which they have preferential hire rights. Please note that Hotel policy requires you to hire employees in these categories who meet the required qualifications you have listed for a position. The benefits of hiring a referred employee are:

— Reducing training and orientation time

— Minimising the loss of staff knowledge and expertise resulting from layoffs and medical separations

— Obtaining a qualified employee who has related campus experience

Referral Process

When a candidate with preferential hire rights is referred to you by a recruiter, you will be required to review the resume and interview the employee if he or she is qualified. Other resumes submitted for your position will not be routed until the SPC candidate is reviewed. Before the recruitment closing date, the recruiter will contact you and route the employee's resume and email you the referral form indicating that you should check references and may review the employee's personnel file. The recruiter will partner with the hiring manager and the candidate (as well as Vocational Rehabilitation as needed) to facilitate the process.

If the employee meets the required qualifications, he or she should be hired. Before making a job offer, you should contact the referring recruiter to verify the employee's previous salary.

If you determine that the referred employee does not meet your required selection criteria, contact the referring recruiter to review your reasons for non-selection. If your reasons are determined to be appropriate, the recruiter will then route all other resumes for your position. You will be asked to provide a written statement of the reasons for non-selection. Please note that you are responsible for notifying the employee of the non-selection and the reasons for non-selection.

Equal Employment Opportunity

Equal Employment Opportunity (EEO) is a term used by the federal government to refer to employment practices that ensure nondiscrimination on the basis of race, sex, religion, color, national origin, physical or mental ability, medical condition, ancestry, or age. The principle behind EEO is that everyone should have the same access to opportunities. EEO is legally mandated for all federal contractors.

Affirmative action is one aspect of the federal government's efforts to ensure equal employment opportunity. The purpose of affirmative action programs is to promote fairness and address the effects of past discrimination in employment by encouraging targeted outreach efforts to attract underutilised minorities and women.

As a supervisor, Equal Employment Opportunity means you:

- provide equal access to all available jobs, training, and promotional opportunities
- provide similar benefits and services to everyone
- apply all policies and practices consistently to applicants and staff
- do not differentiate among applicants or employees on the basis of race, color, national origin, religion, sex, physical or mental disability, medical condition, ancestry, marital status, or age.

In other words, EEO forbids employment discrimination. It requires the elimination of any bias in personnel activities. Affirmative action is a set of specific, results-oriented programs and activities designed to correct underutilisation of minorities and women in the workplace.

Your Role

As a supervisor, you are often faced with pers[illegible] decisions: Should you hire this applicant? Whom should you promote? What corrective action should you take with an employee? Every one of your personnel-related actions is affected by EEO law. If you violate EEO law, the Hotel must bear the responsibility. To prevent such violations, it's not enough to simply know that the law forbids discrimination. You should know the specific kinds of discrimination to avoid in your day-to-day activities with job applicants and staff. Your job involves many different personnel functions, including hiring, training, promotion, termination, and others. Below are examples of actions you can take to fulfill EEO/AA responsibilities:

— Ensure bias-free selection processes by forming diverse selection committees, evaluating candidates on job-related criteria, and completing and maintaining necessary records such as the Interview Data Form.

— Promote accountability for EEO/AA by ensuring that responsibilities in this area are clearly indicated in the applicable job descriptions of managers and supervisors who report to you.

— Evaluate the performance of your supervisory staff in implementing established EEO/AA responsibilities.

— Educate yourself by participating in relevant training and education programs on campus and encouraging subordinate staff with EEO/AA responsibilities to do the same.

— Provide reasonable accommodations such as assistive devices, job restructuring, and site modification for disabled staff members.

— Maintain a hospitable work environment; ethnic jokes and harassment of any kind should not be tolerated.

— Review all personnel activities for potential differential impacts on different groups and unintentional bias in such personnel actions as selection, salary increases, promotion, reclassification, layoff, corrective action, training, and termination.

— Encourage and invest in staff development, ensuring that all staff have access to opportunities.

— Make sure all staff are informed of the Hotel's nondiscrimination policy and the procedures for resolving discrimination complaints.

How to Avoid Complaints

While there is no guaranteed way to avoid employee dissatisfaction with some part of a job, if you follow the above guidelines, the number of complaints can be greatly reduced. Try to look at your affirmative action efforts not as a sero-sum game in which one person's gain is another person's loss, but as an important human resource process that expands opportunities for everyone.

Position Design

A department may wish to create and then recruit for a vacant non- bargaining-unit and non-MSP (Management and Senior Professional) position at more than one level and fill it at the level that best fits its business needs. The range of jobs advertised in this way is called a "career ladder." Most typically, a career ladder consists of a more junior level position and a more experienced level. These levels always differ in the qualifications required, and often by the level of independence and/or complexity of assignments.

Career Ladder Definition

A vacant non-bargaining-unit and non-MSP (Management and Senior Professional) position is advertised at more than one level, to be filled at the level that best fits the department's business needs. Changes in duties and responsibilities can occur with a departmental reorganisation or the assignment of new duties to an existing position. For these reasons, the Compensation Unit continues to review jobs that have changed significantly. For assistance, one should contact the Compensation Consultant assigned to the department.

Job Description

The purposes of a job description are:

— To communicate duties and responsibilities of a position to the employee

— To articulate the essential job duties for Americans with Disabilities Act (ADA) purposes

— To determine the proper classification or grade level for a position

— To describe skills, knowledge, and abilities (KSAs) for recruitment

— To develop hiring specifications

— To design and restructure jobs

— To provide effective employee training and development

— To serve as a basis for performance expectations

The Job Description can take many forms; the recommended form is the Job Description Template, which presents the key information for the purposes listed above. The Job Description Template may be used for all positions on campus, including Management and Senior Profesional (MSP) and information technology (IT) positions. The one exception is for professional support positions in research laboratories, which may continue to be described on the Staff Research Associate questionnaire.

The classification process begins when you submit a new or substantially revised job description with supporting information to the Compensation Unit. Your Compensation Consultant is available to discuss questions you may have before writing the description.

The immediate supervisor or the employee can complete at the job description, depending on which person is more familiar with the position. If the incumbent is new to the job or the position is new, you may wish to complete the job description. If the employee completes it, you should validate it, because you are the person with authority to determine the actual duties and responsibilities of the position.

Some departments or control units have personnel managers who review the job description, compare it to positions within the department and provide guidance on reclassification requests; they may also have delegated authority to classify positions.

Job Description Template

A well-written job description should be easily understood by anyone who reads it - not only by those familiar with the position. Some technical abbreviations, language, or documentation unique to the unit may be quite understandable when used within the unit, but might require further explanation for classification. When writing a job description, always be clear, concise, and complete.

A results-oriented description explains why functions are performed and allows you to more effectively manage the objectives of the position; it also helps the Compensation Consultant evaluate the position more quickly and effectively. Remember to develop the following in the job description:

— *Organisation Summary*: A brief description of your unit so those reviewing the position know the context within which it operates.
— *Purpose of the Position*: A brief description of the overall purpose of the position, telling why it exists.

Classification Factors

Independence/Supervision Received: Check the box that best describes the kind of supervision given to the position and expand upon how the position is supervised as necessary. Tell from whom and in what form the assignments are received, and what kinds of instruction and directions are given. For example, what work is performed independently and what work is routed to you for review?

Scope and Impact: Describe the organisational scope of the position. What part of the campus is affected by the position's work—department? What is the primary constituency? What are the consequences of the position's actions on the group?

Problem-solving and Decision-making: Describe the kinds of problems to be resolved and the planning that is required of the position. Identify the authority and/or responsibility to make decisions, develop and revise procedures, make official commitments, etc. Indicate to whom recommendations are made and for whom analyses are performed and reports are prepared.

Major Functions: Identify the major functions and duties (those that require at least 10% of time over a specific time period such as annually, monthly, weekly). Use specific action verbs to describe duties; for example, "open, post and distribute mail," not "handle mail." Avoid vague terms like "assist in", "arrange for", or "administer," which do not describe job duties.

Indicate essential duties: A job function is considered essential if:

— Performance of the function is the reason for the job existing.

— A limited number of employees are capable of performing the function.

— The function is highly specialised, requiring unique expertise or abilities.

Supervision Exercised: If supervisory responsibilities are assigned, explain the employee's role; for example: interview and select employees; train; plan, schedule, and assign work; evaluate performance; and take disciplinary action. Be precise and specific in identifying all supervisory tasks.

Knowledge, Skills, Abilities, and Other Requirements: Describe the kind of knowledge required (of Hotel procedures, policies or of a professional field, or other specialised body of knowledge), the specialised skills and abilities as well as other requirements such as licenses, certifications.

Addendum: Information Technology Positions: Complete the Addendum for IT Positions for Programmer/Analyst, Computing Resource Manager and other information technology (IT) titles. Describe the key required technical knowledge and skills and the technical environment of the position.

Signatures: The job description should be signed by the employee, supervisor and manager and a copy kept in the departmental files. The signatures certify to the accuracy of the assigned duties and responsibilities. If a supervisor wishes to note any exceptions to the job description, they should be appended to the description with a copy to the employee.

Completing the Classification Request Form

The supervisor should attach the completed Job Description Template to the Classification Request Form and address the following:

Significant changes to the position since last review: Identify specific areas of change. This section is extremely valuable for the Compensation Consultant's review. The more information you provide on relevant changes, the more easily the Compensation Consultant can make an informed decision. If you have a copy of the duties previously performed, attach it to the description.

Recommendations: Your reasons for recommending a reclassification and/or title change should be noted in the cover letter.

Preparing an Organisation Chart

Submit a current organisation chart with each classification/reclassification request. A formal printed organisation chart is not required, but it should be sufficiently detailed to reflect departmental structure and the position's relationship in the current organisation.

Physical, Environmental, and Mental Demands Form (PEM)

This form helps a department determine the demands of a position and recognise any accommodations that may be necessary under the Americans with Disabilities Act (ADA). A copy of the PEM form should be attached to the Job Description in the employee's personnel file. For Requisitions, document any outstanding PEMs or any PEMs unusual for the classification. The PEM forms are available from Campus Supply, in the Office of Human Resources and on-line at.

Reasons for Classification Review

When developing your reasons for the classification review, ask yourself whether the duties and level of responsibility have changed significantly. Normally, descriptions are not submitted for review unless they have changed substantially and significantly since the last review. If you are uncertain, you can discuss the changes with your Compensation Consultant.

Sometimes a reclassification request is motivated by the desire to reward a top performer. When an employee exceeds performance standards, you may feel pressure to show appreciation through reclassification. Such efforts are more appropriately recognised through the merit program. In special circumstances, an equity increase might be appropriate.

It is extremely important to request a job review only when appropriate and to thoroughly prepare your request, including determining whether budget dollars are available to fund a salary increase resulting from the reclassification, if approved. Ill-conceived reclassification requests that are denied can be de-motivating and can become a source of conflict when the employee feels that the supervisor did not fully support the reclassification request.

A reclassification is normally effective on the first of the month following receipt of the request in the Office of Human Resources

Job Evaluation

When reviewing a position for classification, the Compensation Consultant carefully studies the job description and other related materials such as the organisation charts submitted for review. Such documents highlight important information related to changes in the position.

The Consultant considers how a position has changed (additional duties, supervision exercised and received, and other critical components of the position) and compares the position to the published classification standards for the job series and to similar positions at Berkeley.

In some cases, the Consultant will consult with campus experts in the field to obtain their perspective and assessment of the position. Decisions regarding the classification of positions in the MSP program are made by the Vice Chancellors. A job series or job family is a group of jobs with similar functions that require similar specialised knowledge and skills.

The job classification guidelines identify the different levels of work within a series. Some job classification guidelines have been developed specifically for the Berkeley campus, while others are used across the entire UC system. Compensation Consultants consider these important factors when classifying a position:

— Nature or type of work performed
— Level of responsibility
— Impact of position on the unit, department, or campus
— Reporting relationships
— Scope of duties
— Complexity of work
— Creativity/innovation
— Supervision received
— Supervision exercised
— Knowledge and skills required to perform the duties
— Other factors cannot be considered in classifying a position:
— Performance of the incumbent
— Longevity of the incumbent in position

— Qualifications of the incumbent that are not required by the position
— Personality

Financial Needs

Based on the review and comparisons, the Compensation Consultant determines the appropriate title. The Consultant may call you during the course of the review to discuss the findings. You will receive written confirmation of the decision, usually through email.

Appeals and Reviews

Check the relevant personnel policy or contract for guidelines on formally appealing or reviewing a classification decision.

Compensation Unit Resources

Consulting with departments on reorganisations and position design, including determining more appropriate and cost effective structuring of jobs to meet unit needs.

Consulting on salary setting and salary increase criteria. Designing and implementing effective classification methodologies for the campus. Classifying and reclassifying positions in the various personnel programs. Providing information on how to write job descriptions. Consulting on how changes in duties may affect a job. Providing campus liaison with the Office of the President on major classification and compensation issues.

Salary Ranges

Salary ranges involve a number of factors: local, state, or

national prevailing salary rates, campus recruiting and retention problems, and internal relationships to other related classifications.

Currently, two different salary structures for staff positions exist in the campus system: positions with steps (step-based) and positions without steps (open ranges). You can find out which structure a particular position is in by checking the contract or policy that covers the position, or by looking the title up in the Berkeley Campus Title and Pay Plan. If the position has steps, they will show in the Title and Pay Plan. If no step rates appear, then the position does not have steps.

Positions with Steps

Covered under some collective bargaining unit contracts and Police Sergeants covered by PPSM.

— The salary of an employee must be on one of the predefined steps.

— *Title and Pay Plan* consists of ranges of monthly and hourly rates of pay

— A Step Structure *may range from 1 to 25 or more steps of pay, and may or may not include half-steps.*

— Salaries for the majority of staff employees are stated in monthly rates.

— With a range adjustment, each step is increased by a specific percentage and each employee on a step automatically receives the new rate for that step.

Positions Without Steps

Those in the PPSM - Managers and Senior Professionals (MSP) group and PPSM - Professional and Support Staff (PSS), except for Police Sergeants, and some positions covered under some collective bargaining unit contracts.

— A *salary grade range* is assigned for each title in MSP & PSS.

— Salaries of individuals in MSP program are determined by their placement in the appropriate range.

— Each grade range is divided into *quartiles* with a defined minimum, midpoint, and maximum rate. There is a percent range spread within each grade and approximately a 10% midpoint differential between grades in most cases.

— *Salaries are stated in* annual rates *and in whole dollar amounts, not steps.*

— An individual's salary may be any whole dollar amount within the range.

Range Adjustments and Structure Adjustments

Salary range adjustments apply to step-based positions, usually in one or more selected classifications on a systemwide or local campus basis. Recommendations for salary range adjustments are based on, but not necessarily limited to:

— Prevailing salaries in public jurisdictions and private industry

— Campus recruiting and retention problems

— Internal comparisons

— Amount of available funding

— Agreements with unions

Open-Range or Merit-Based Pay

Salary structures for open-range or merit-based pay plans are reviewed annually and adjusted when funding is available from the state and/or when warranted by market conditions. Automatic increases are not provided when structure is adjusted; individuals are usually eligible for performance-based or merit-based increases.

Salary Placement Guidelines

The Salary Placement Guidelines are intended to provide managers with the framework they need to establish and maintain fair and equitable salaries in managing the work force. These guidelines apply to new hire, promotional, reclassification, stipend, equity, and merit increase salary actions. These Salary Placement Guidelines apply to the broad salary ranges, which do not have steps and which allow managers to appoint employees at a specific whole dollar amount.

— *First Quartile* (from the minimum up to halfway to the midpoint of the range): The first quartile of the range is usually intended for individuals who are new to the grade, are in a learning situation, and/or do not have substantial experience in the new position.
— *Second Quartile: The second quartile of the range is intended for employees who have gained experience and skill and who are becoming more proficient in the position for which they were hired. They generally meet expectations in their positions.*
— *Third Quartile: The third quartile is typically reserved for experienced employees who frequently exceed expectations.*
— *Fourth Quartile: The fourth quartile of the range is normally reserved for individuals who are consistently exceptional performers and who have extensive experience.*

Starting Salaries/New Hire Salaries

Establishing a starting salary for a new employee or deciding to give a promotional increase requires careful consideration. In both cases, you should determine how the employee's prior experience, knowledge, and skills compare with other employees already performing the same job.

Before establishing the starting salary of a new employee, consider each of the following factors:

— Recruiting difficulty (size of qualified applicant pool, length of recruitment, etc.)
— Candidate's salary expectations
— Comparable internal salaries
— Employee's knowledge, skills, and experience compared to others performing similar work
— Budget

For positions with steps (those covered under some bargaining contracts and Police Sergeants in PPSM):

— Authority up to the midpoint of the range is delegated to the hiring department. The Vice Chancellor or delegated Dean has approval through the range. Consultation with OHR is expected for above midpoint salaries. For PPSM-MSP, PPSM-PSS positions and some positions covered under some collective bargaining unit contracts:
— Requests for consideration above the midpoint are approved by the Vice Chancellor, except where this authority is re-delegated to specific Deans. MSP appointments above the midpoint of the salary range require final approval by the appropriate Vice Chancellor.
— Consultation with OHR is expected for salaries above midpoint.

Promotional and Reclassification Increases

For positions under PPSM, hiring departments are authorised to grant promotional and reclassification increases, not to exceed 25% total in the fiscal year (except as required to reach range minimum).

— For exclusively represented employees in units with collective bargaining contracts, consult the contract for the specific authority to grant promotional increases.

For noncompetitive lateral moves, normally there will be no change in salary. For a lateral move into a competitively recruited position, a salary increase may be granted based on the qualifications of the employee and the requirements of the position.

Merit Increases

Salary increases are granted to eligible employees in career positions based upon their job performance. Merit eligibility is contingent upon completing three months of service in PPSM. The amount of the increase depends upon the individual's performance in relation to current pay and assigned responsibilities, position within salary range, performance relative to other members of the review unit, and availability of funds.

The Compensation Unit manages the campus' merit programs. Key elements of the staff merit process typically are:

— The Compensation Unit sends a call letter to the control units (organisations under a Vice Chancellor or Provost), announcing the merit program and outlining the merit increase guidelines and control figures as determined by the campus within parameters set by the Office of the President. (Control figures represent the fund pool available for merit increases.)

— Higher merit increases are provided for employees who perform above expectation in achieving goals and objectives; however, no merit increase may result in the final salary exceeding the range maximum and no salary is to fall below the range minimum.

Administrative Stipends/Temporary Reclassifications

Under PPSM, stipends may be granted to recognise temporary performance of higher-level duties or "other significant duties" not part of the employee's regular position. For employees represented by a collective bargaining contract, consult with the contract to determine stipend/temporary reclassification constraints.

Equity Increases

An equity increase is typically based on a salary inequity that cannot be corrected through the merit review cycle. A salary inequity exists when an employee's salary is significantly below that of others in the same title code with similar performance, experience, skills, knowledge, and assignments. Examples of situations that may indicate a salary inequity include:

— The salary of a long term-employee is low relative to a new hire whose salary is market-driven.

— Significant salary compression exists between a supervisor and his/her employees.

— An employee changes from a limited to a career position in the same class.

— Market factors influence recruitment and retention.

An equity increase may also be considered for employees taking on higher-level functions that do not warrant reclassification to a higher salary grade.

New Employee Orientation

An effective orientation will:

— Foster an understanding of the campus culture, its values, and its diversity
— Help the new employee make a successful adjustment to the new job
— Help the new employee understand her role and how she fits into the total organisation
— Help the new employee achieve objectives and shorten the learning curve
— Help the new employee develop a positive working relationship by building a foundation of knowledge about campus mission, objectives, policies, organisation structure, and functions

6

Performance Management

Performance management is an ongoing process of communication between a supervisor and an employee that occurs throughout the year, in support of accomplishing the strategic objectives of the organisation. The communication process includes clarifying expectations, setting objectives, identifying goals, providing feedback, and evaluating results.

Management of Employee Performance

The Performance management process is a cycle, with discussions varying year-to-year based on changing objectives. The cycle includes planning, checking-in, and assessment

— To begin the planning process, you and your employee review overall expectations, which includes collaborating on the development of performance objectives. Individual development goals are also updated. You then develop a performance plan that directs the employee's efforts toward achieving specific results to support organisational excellence and employee success.

— Goals and objectives are discussed throughout the year, during check-in meetings. This provides a framework to ensure employees achieve results through coaching and mutual feedback.

— At the end of the performance period, you assess the employee's performance against expected objectives, as well as the means used and behaviours demonstrated in achieving those objectives. Together, you establish new objectives for the next performance period.

To perform well, employees need to know what is expected of them. The starting point is an *up-to-date job description* that describes the essential functions, tasks, and responsibilities of the job. It also outlines the general areas of knowledge and skills required of the employee an employee to be successful in the job.

Performance expectations go beyond the job description. When you think about high quality on-the-job performance, you are really thinking about a range of expected job outcomes, such as,

— What goods and services should the job produce?

— What impact should the work have on the organisation?

— How do you expect the employee to act with clients, colleagues, and supervisors?

— What are the organisational values the employee must demonstrate?

— What are the processes, methods, or means the employee is expected to use?

The range of performance expectations can be broad but can generally be broken into two categories:

— Results (The goods and services produced by an employee often measured by objectives or standards)

— Actions & Behaviours (The methods and means used to make a product and the behaviours and values demonstrated during the process. Actions and Behaviours can be measured through performance dimensions.)

Performance expectations serve as a foundation for communicating about performance throughout the year. They also serve as the basis for assessing employee performance. When you and an employee set clear expectations about the results that must be achieved and the methods or approaches needed to achieve them, you establish a path for success.

Performance Objectives and Standards

Performance objectives and standards are two of the most common methods to define expected results. Both objectives and standards are most useful when, in addition to being written down and verifiable, they are:

— Specific – Objectives and standards should let employees know exactly which actions and results they are expected to accomplish.

— Measurable – Whenever possible, objectives and standards should be based on quantitative measures such as direct counts, percentages, and ratios..

— Attainable – The objective or standard should be achievable, but challenging.

— Reasonable – An employee should be able to meet expected results with the resources available.

— Timely – Results should be delivered within a time period that meets the department and organisation's needs.

Objectives and standards identify baselines for measuring performance results. From performance objectives and standards, supervisors can provide specific feedback describing the gap between expected and actual performance.

It can be very useful to define both objectives and standards for a position, but it is not necessary. Standards are directly linked to job-task completion. *Example*: Ensure that all grant requests are written, reviewed, and submitted to the granting agency/foundation by the required deadlines.

Objectives are broader in scope, go beyond day-to-day standards, and are clearly linked to helping the organisation or department meet its goals and objectives. *Example*: Identify three new grant/funding sources by the end of FY 2006.

In some cases, you and the employee may find it better to set a series of standards with only a few objectives, while in other situations it may make more sense to set objectives alone.

Characteristics of objectives

A performance objective is a future state of achievement that helps the organisation succeed and create value. It is a direct link between the work an employee does and the department and organisation's overall objectives and mission. As the organisation's needs change and direction shifts, so will an employee's performance objectives.

— Performance objectives express mutually understood agreements for results that an employee is expected to produce *during the performance assessment period*.

— Performance objectives are not separate from an employee's job, but part of the job.

— Performance objectives are "ends" towards which you and your employee direct effort and focus resources.

For these reasons it is best not to dictate objectives, but set them through discussion, negotiation, compromise, and agreement. While much has been written about differences between objectives, targets, and goals, there are no real differences.

Objectives

Objectives force you and the employee to think of planning for *results*, not just planning *activities*. Identifying objectives encourages you and the employee to continually look for ways to improve overall department effectiveness and efficiency, and link individual and departmental operations and results to the overall planning and mission of the Hotel. Objectives set through a collaborative process between the employee, supervisor, and department elicit commitment.

Expressing performance objectives

The following questions may help generate ideas for performance objectives. Based on departmental/unit objectives:

— What can this employee do to improve the overall effectiveness of the work unit?

— Has the employee suggested programme or process changes that help us meet our objectives and can be completed during the appraisal period?

— What needs to be done to improve the quality of our service? What refinements can we make to our operations? What needs to be introduced or eliminated?

— What are we ready to do now that we could not do last year (due to increased resources, system modifications, changed priorities, updated skills, etc.)?

— What skills, processes, products must be updated to meet client demand?

Considerations when developing objectives

You and the employee should develop objectives together whenever possible.

— Set short-term goals with a long-term view. Objectives are generally set for periods of a year or less, which may sacrifice long-term gain to generate results in the short-term.

— Identify critical issues and possible obstacles

— Do not underestimate resource needs.

— Build in flexibility. Regular status update and check-in meetings make it much easier to identify problems or shifts in unit priorities and change course.

Characteristics of Performance Standards

Standards describe the conditions that must exist before the performance can be rated satisfactory. Performance standards are approved expressions of the,

— Performance threshold(s),

— Requirement(s), or

— Expectation(s)

A standard focuses on task completion. It is specifically tied to duties/responsibilities. A performance standard should:

— Be realistic, in other words, attainable by any qualified, competent, and fully trained person who has the authority and resources to achieve the desired result

— Be "exceedable." Employees should know that they can and should exceed expectations. Standards should not be used as an excuse to maintain the status quo if change is needed.

— Describe the conditions that exist when performance meets expectations

— Be expressed in terms of quantity, quality, time, cost, effect, manner of performance, or method of doing
— Be measurable, with specified method(s) of gathering performance data and measuring performance against standards

Expressing standards

The terms for expressing performance standards are outlined below:

— *Quantity*: specifies how much work must be completed within a certain period of time, e.g., enters 30 enrollments per day.
— *Quality*: describes how well the work must be accomplished. Specifies accuracy, precision, appearance, or effectiveness, e.g., 95% of documents submitted are accepted without revision.
— *Timeliness*: answers the questions: By when, how soon, or within what period, e.g., all work orders completed within five working days of receipt.
— *Effective Use of Resources*: used when performance can be assessed in terms of utilisation of resources: money saved, waste reduced, etc., e.g., the computer handbook project will be completed with only internal resources.
— *Effects of Effort*: addresses the ultimate effect to be obtained; expands statements of effectiveness by using phrases such as: so that, in order to, or as shown by, e.g., establish inventory levels for storeroom so that supplies are maintained 100% of the time.
— *Manner of Performance*: describes conditions in which an individual's personal behaviour has an effect on performance, e.g., assists other employees in the work unit in accomplishing assignments.

— *Method of Performing Assignments*: describes requirements; used when only the officially-prescribed policy, procedure, or rule for accomplishing the work is acceptable, e.g., 100A Forms are completed in accordance with established office procedures.

Performance standards for key areas of responsibility

Write performance standards for each key area of responsibility on the employee's job description. Focus on tasks that have the greatest importance; *it is not necessary to write standards for every task.* Standards are usually established when an assignment is made, and should be reviewed if the employee's job description is updated. Whenever possible, have employees participate in developing standards. The discussion of standards should include the criteria for achieving satisfactory performance and the proof of performance (methods you will use to gather information about work performance).

In departments where more than one person does the same task or function, standards may be written for the parts of the jobs that are the same and applied to all positions doing that task. Remember, changes in performance standards may require notice for represented employees. CUE, for example requires notice. In addition, there are contracts that cover specialised professions, such as Nurses and Police, that have their own standard-setting and evaluation processes.

Performance Dimensions

In addition to objectives and standards (which focus on end results) it is important to consider other aspects of performance.

Understanding the actions and behaviours that employees can use to perform the job is often as important to success as end results. Behaviour is the day-to-day activity in which people engage to produce results and relates closely to the process side of work.

Focusing on the way people go about their work is based on the belief that doing things correctly will lead to positive organisational results. However, many actions and behaviours are not easy to measure. For this reason, managers and employees should discuss difficult to quantify aspects of performance in terms that are

— Specific,

— Observable,

— Job-related, and

— Behavioural.

When described in this way, behaviours and actions can be grouped into *performance* dimensions that can be used to assess job performance. For example, if success in meeting an objective such as "updating an on-line graduate application programme" requires strong interpersonal skills, then the employee should know that s/he will have to build solid relationships, collaborate, and incorporate ideas and suggestions made by colleagues. Performance will be assessed on how well behaviours associated with the dimension, interpersonal skills, are demonstrated in reaching the objective.

Characteristics of performance dimensions

Performance dimensions are defined based on the job and the work itself. In creating a performance dimension you start with the job and state the range of behaviours employees must exhibit to successfully meet or exceed job expectations. These behaviours are then grouped into broad categories that we are calling "dimensions." Performance dimensions help answer the question: "How does someone act and/or behave when s/he does the job well?"

Since dimensions are broad categories, a specific dimension generally applies to any employee working in a given job. It is also possible for departments and units and even entire organisations to have dimensions that apply to any employee who works in the group.

In addition to strong interpersonal skills, other examples of performance dimensions include:

— Customer Service Orientation
— Teamwork
— Effective Communication
— Valuing Diversity
— Analysis and Problem-Solving
— Decision-Making and Results Orientation
— Adaptability
— Fostering a Safe and Secure Environment

This list is by no means exhaustive. Each organisation should agree on the definitions used for a dimension and the job or job groups to which a dimension will be applied. It is common, for example, to have a series of dimensions that apply to all supervisors and/or managers in an organisation. The definition and validation of dimensions is a key objective of the Staff Infrastructure Steering Committee (SISC) Performance Management Working Group.

Expressing performance dimensions

For dimensions to be an effective means of measuring performance, they must have two characteristics:

— Have a clear general definition, and

— Have well-defined levels of performance at each point along a rating scale.

The Teamwork is one example of a performance dimension definition.

The Teamwork Dimension describes how employees build alliances to solve problems and achieve objectives, work cooperatively and respectively with co-workers, use diplomacy and tact when interacting with others, diffuse tension, help manage conflict, collaborate, foster collegial and cooperative attitudes, relate well to all kinds of people regardless of level inside or outside of organisation, and contribute to the overall success of their work units and departments by sharing knowledge and information.

Performance dimensions and competencies

Performance dimensions focus on the actions that need to be taken by anyone doing that job to get the work done. As discussed above, performance dimensions are groupings of behaviours/actions and are defined based on the requirements and expectations of the job.

In contrast, a competency is a cluster of knowledge, skills and abilities that describes a general trait that an employee has or should have to perform a job. While competencies relate to the individual, performance dimensions relate to the job. For example, a performance dimension for a Budget Analyst's position may be to "Prepare budget documents and reports." It will then be useful to measure how well an employee holding the job:

— "Presents information in a clear, concise manner that illustrates budget issues that need to be resolved",

— "Produces timely budget documents and reports that are tailored to each customer's needs. And,

— Frequently uses graphics and other aids to summarise and synthesise data.

If the person holding the position is a highly competent communicator and knowledgeable about the budget process, then there is an overlap between the performance dimension "Prepare budget documents and reports" and the employee's "communication" and "technical knowledge" competencies. Since competencies focus on an employee's traits they are useful in hiring and development. Performance dimensions, which focus on the job, are useful for performance management and assessment.

Performance Expectations

Put expectations in writing

A written summary of your discussions during the planning process serves as a record of your mutually understood expectations. Putting expected results (objectives and standards) and expected actions/ behaviours (performance dimensions) in writing is useful when

— Allocating resources,

— Discussing budgets, and

— Prioritising programmes.

Mutually developed written expectations also help focus feedback and minimise ambiguity when it is time to assess results.

Verify expectations

Performance expectations should be verifiable. Early in the performance management cycle, you, with input from the employee, should identify how and where evidence about the employee's performance will be gathered.

Measurable (quantitative) expectations are the easiest ones to verify. Frequently, however, expectations cannot be put into measurable terms easily or accurately. At this point, consider developing qualitative expectations, which can generally be made verifiable by spelling out the criteria to be fulfilled, behaviours to be demonstrated, and/or target dates to be met.

Specifying how performance expectations will be verified at the time the responsibility is assigned helps employees keep track of their progress and makes check-in meetings and performance status updates much more focused and efficient.

There are many ways to verify performance; some of the most common are:

- — Specific work products (tangible evidence that can be reviewed without the employee being present)
- — Reports and records, such as attendance, safety, inventory, financial records, etc.
- — Checklists that can be completed by a client or supervisor listing specific, observable criteria that need to be met in order for an expectation to be considered complete. Criteria usually require a "yes" or "no" answer, such as: "implement a new programme by [x] date."
- — Direct observation
- — Rating scales that define, as precisely as possible, behaviours at different levels of performance (behaviourally anchored rating scales).
- — Commendations or constructive or critical comments received about the employee's work

Around the Office

In addition to the job description and the performance

standards you establish for your employees, other tools help them do their jobs. These tools can consist of a desk manual, work rules, guidelines on office procedures, and personnel files. Job aids such as these can:

— Provide continuity and equity in the workplace when implementing policies and procedures
— Allow the employee to operate with some independence
— Free your time for other management responsibilities

Desk manuals

Desk manuals can be a great resource for employees, especially if you have several employees performing similar tasks, or if certain tasks must be performed in a specific way. Desk manuals can be developed by you and/or your employee and should be easily accessible. Set time aside for updating the manual as necessary.

The manual should include:

— Instructions on how to use the manual
— Definitions of procedures or processes
— Information about when and where to get help
— Other resources and references

Work Rules

Many rules are already in place in the form of policies, contracts, procedures, regulations, laws, and mandates. These rules determine the actions of the Hotel, departments, and employees, and actions to be taken by you as a supervisor. Work rules may be needed for direct guidance for employees, covering their day-to-day responsibilities outside specific, work-related performance standards for their position. If you are establishing new work rules or changing existing work rules, the Labour Relations Unit in Human Resources must notify the appropriate exclusive representative, such as AFSCME.

Establishing Work Rules

Work rules should be:

— *Necessary*. Is there a need for clearly defined, written work rules?

— *Reasonable*. Rules should make supervision easier.

— In compliance with existing policy, contracts, and laws.

— Beneficial to your employees as they conduct the department's business.

— *Clear*. There should be no question about the intent of the language.

— *Enforceable*. Be willing to enforce the work rules after they are established.

— *Publicised*. Posted on departmental bulletin boards, covered in staff meetings, distributed to each employee, and made part of an employee's orientation and information packet.

Rules of Work Rules

Follow these guidelines to make your work rules as effective as possible:

— DO. Write for a specific job category or location such as service, clerical, front desk, grounds.

— DO. Consult with your Employee Relations Specialist so you get off on the right track.

— DO. Write rules that are practical for you to monitor.

— DO. Make sure you are willing to apply them evenly to ALL employees in the job category.

— DO. Be prepared to provide oral communications to employees who may have reading or language difficulties.
— DO. Review after contract negotiations or policy revisions to ensure rules comply with the contract or policy.
— DON'T. Repeat a law, policy, or contract.
— DON'T. Violate a law, policy, or contract.
— DON'T. Include performance standards in work rules.
— DON'T. Use wording that is vague.
— DON'T. Institute verbal work rules.
— DON'T. Phase in rules after they are issued; start enforcing them on the effective date.

Sample department work rules

Proper Notice for Sick Leave: Employees must call their immediate supervisor or designated contact within thirty minutes of their beginning work time if they will be absent due to illness or other unforeseen circumstances. Exceptions to this rule will be considered on an individual basis.

Use of Department Vehicle: Employees must have a valid California driver's license, must be on department business, and should reserve the car at least one day in advance. Reservations are on a first come, first served basis. The employee is responsible for obeying traffic regulations.

Break Periods: Breaks should be taken at the work site in predesignated areas. Employees who wish to leave the work site must receive permission from their immediate supervisor or manager.

Equipment, Supplies, and other Hotel Property: No department supplies and equipment are to be taken out of the building for personal use. Abuse, misuse, or theft of supplies or equipment, or defacement or abuse of Hotel property will result in disciplinary and/or legal action.

Hours of work

A work schedule is the normal hours of work on specific days within a 40-hour work week. Work hours for employees, including salaried and hourly employees, are based on a schedule determined by you. Scheduling work hours includes work days, starting and stopping time, lunches, and breaks. When you are establishing work hours:

— Make sure they comply with policies and contracts.

— Schedule and control them. If you make a change you should consult with the appropriate policy or contract for notice procedures.

— Authorise overtime and keep accurate records. Process payment of overtime promptly.

Flexible work arrangements

A variety of flexible work arrangements are permitted under personnel policies and collective bargaining agreements. Many departments have successfully incorporated variations on the traditional 8:00 to 5:00 with lunch from noon to 1:00 schedule. Alternative possibilities are wide-ranging, and include:

— fixed full-time schedules, such as arriving at 7:30 a.m. and leaving at 4:00 p.m., with a half-hour for lunch

— flexible schedules centering on a fixed core, such as varying arrival time between 7:00 a.m. and 9:00 a.m. and departure time between 4:00 p.m. and 6:00 p.m.

- — compressed work weeks of fewer than five days, such as working
- — four 10-hour days
- — part-time work
- — job shares (a form of part-time work)
- — part-year work, such as 9-, 10-, and 11-month career appointments with corresponding 3-, 2- or 1-month periods of furlough each year
- — telecommuting, in which the employee works at home or at an alternate work site part of each week and communicates by phone or by other electronic means

Advantages of flexible work arrangements

The Chancellor encourages you to give serious consideration to employee requests for alternative work arrangements, because flexibility can enable employees to resolve conflicts between their responsibilities at work and at home. By helping employees integrate their personal concerns with their work concerns, you can benefit in the following ways:

- — Improved productivity and morale
- — Stronger ability to recruit and retain the best employees
- — Better economy and efficiency of operations (as when staffing varies based on peaks and valleys of activity, or space is freed up as a result of telecommuting)
- — A more creative and motivating work environment

Evaluating requests

Although flexible arrangements are encouraged, they are not an employee right. You have the approval authority, and should only approve requests that will not be detrimental to your departmental operations. Many times, however, a request that may at first seem unworkable turns out to be quite feasible after careful study and perhaps some minor adjustments. For example, an employee may want to arrive at 7:00 and leave at 4:00, yet you know the services which the employee provides must continue to be available until 5:00. Perhaps another employee in the unit prefers to work a late schedule, arriving at 9:00 and leaving at 6:00. By approving both schedules in tandem, you may actually be able to extend the department's hours from 7:00 to 6:00, and thus improve service.

Your Employee Relations Specialist can help you review employee requests to look for ways to maintain departmental operations and minimise liability. For example, you will need to assure that employees who are eligible for premium overtime do not actually work more than 40 hours in a week. Telecommuting arrangements in particular present a number of liability issues, which your Employee Relations Specialist can help you minimise.

Attendance

Employees are expected to be at work on time; they are also responsible for notifying their supervisors when they will be absent because they are ill or for other unexpected reasons. An unacceptable number of absences or tardiness may result in disciplinary action up to and including dismissal. Following are some guidelines for attendance:

— Keep accurate and current records.

— Let your employees know what is expected of them in regard to attendance and punctuality.

— Review your employees' attendance records. This will give you a chance for corrective counseling or to commend employees who have outstanding attendance records.

— Ensure that vacation leave, compensatory time off, and alternate holidays off are scheduled and taken at the convenience of the department.

— Review requests for time off for personal reasons in advance when possible. When deciding whether to grant the request, consider the operating needs of your unit and the reason for the request.

— Take appropriate disciplinary action when an employee abuses attendance standards.

— Report all absences accurately and as soon as possible to ensure proper payment.

Personnel files

The proper handling of personnel records or personnel files in departments often raises questions. The campus keeps only personnel records that are relevant and necessary to the administration of personnel programmes. These records should be maintained with accuracy, relevance, timeliness, and completeness, and appropriate and reasonable safeguards should be established to ensure security and confidentiality.

Delegation

Delegation is a way to appropriately and consistently provide direction to the staff. By delegating properly, you can teach employees new skills and expertise to help them be more productive and instill a sense of self-reliance, improving morale and motivation. As a supervisor, you must assess your staff's current abilities and their potential to accept and complete assignments through established guidelines. You must know how to plan and coordinate a variety of activities and how to monitor progress. Delegation brings into play many management functions planning, organising, co-ordinating, motivating, communicating, and leading.

Your goals in delegating are to:

- Provide opportunities for growth and development
- Empower staff by letting them be responsible for the work
- Increase morale and self-confidence
- Give yourself more time to concentrate on staff and other management issues
- Enhance creativity and skills
- Increase staff involvement and commitment to the job

Resistance to delegation

Understanding why you may be reluctant to delegate tasks and why staff members may be reluctant to accept them will help you be a more effective delegator. The reluctance to delegate tasks is understandable because you still retain accountability. Sometimes you may feel the transfer of a task involves a certain degree of risk. Your staff may also be thinking about the risk; they are afraid that they may be criticised if they fail. Some common reasons why managers and supervisors avoid delegation are:

- They are afraid the employee may make mistakes
- They think it takes too much time to delegate
- They feel that completing the task themselves would be more efficient
- They are concerned about losing control
- They fear that employees will resent delegation

Choosing projects or tasks to delegate

Choose the projects and tasks you delegate carefully to

make sure you are balancing the risk with the potential rewards. You may want to delegate tasks that meet the following criteria:

— All necessary information is available to your employee

— The parameters are clear

— The task does not involve responsibilities traditionally associated with management (i.e., hiring, performance appraisals, disciplinary action)

Preparing employees for delegation

— Find out what employees already know about the task. With this knowledge, you can communicate more efficiently, without losing employees' attention or insulting their intelligence.

— Give a reason why explanation. Employees who understand the purpose of projects tend to commit themselves more fully to completing those projects.

— Provide an example or illustration of the task.

— Make it clear that you welcome questions. Employees may feel embarrassed or afraid to reveal their lack of knowledge about a subject or task. Reassure them that you are happy to answer any questions they might have.

— Work with employees at the beginning of new projects to provide the encouragement and instruction they need.

Making delegation effective

You can do several things to increase your effectiveness in delegation. For delegation to work, your staff must have a clear understanding of their responsibilities, the extent of their authority, and the results that they are expected to produce.

- Select the employees who have the ability to do the job according to their experience and knowledge.
- Make sure your expectations are clearly understood.
- Let employees know you believe in their ability to carry out the task.
- Clearly define the employees' authority and responsibility.
- Monitor progress and establish feedback mechanisms.
- Establish deadlines and milestones.
- Empower employees by giving them the latitude to use their own imagination and initiative.
- Reward employees for the positive results they produce.
- Provide constructive feedback.

Managing Reorganisations

When changes occur in your department's programmes, staffing patterns, or resources, you may want to take a close look at possible reorganisation. Since reorganisations can raise some of the same issues as layoffs.

Steps in managing a reorganisation

- Define the problem.
- Determine whether existing jobs and structures are meeting department goals.
- Consider what factors contribute to effectiveness of jobs and structure.

— Identify methods for collecting input from staff.
— Verbal, written, and computer surveys
— Problem-solving teams
— Review committees
— Identify a new structure or model that will support your goals, including:
— Distribution of functions throughout the organisation (definition of functions to be performed, groupings of functions, and the relationships among functions)
— Vertical and horizontal authority relationships
— Communication/decision-making process (how formal decisions are made and by whom, and the information system established for decision-making)
— Internal departmental policies (the decisions, rules, or guidelines established in production, personnel, purchasing, research and development, and other areas)
— The attributes of department employees (includes abilities, skills, experience, and other behavioural issues)
— Develop a reorganisation proposal, including:
— Timeframe
— Reasons for reorganisation
— Before and after organisation charts
— Job descriptions for new, changed positions
— Names, titles of employees to be affected by changed or eliminated jobs, new reporting lines, physical relocation, or reduction in time
— Review of Affirmative Action impact
— Order of potential layoffs for career positions based on seniority points

— Notices to go to unions
— A communication plan
— Identify the different groups who will need communication and the different messages/information they will need
— Determine series of review and update meetings with management
— Determine schedule of informational meetings with staff
— Plan communications outside department to announce reorganisation
— Set up individual meetings with employees projected for layoff and for those employees whose jobs will change significantly
— Determine skills needed for each position.
— Compare current skills with what is needed.
— Determine training needs and resources.
— Design and implement training.
— Review, reassess, and gather input during implementation.
— Determine methods to get feedback during implementation.
— Include systems that will provide regular feedback from management, staff, and client groups.
— Build an effective team
— Clarify mission, goals, and standards for success.
— Schedule regular staff meetings.
— Facilitate communication by remaining open to suggestions and concerns.
— Act as harmonising influence by looking for opportunities to mediate and resolve minor disputes.

— Encourage all team members to share information.

— Support brainstorming and consensus decision-making where appropriate.

Resistance to reorganisation can be greater when:

— The purpose of the reorganisation is not clear. When employees don't understand why changes are implemented, anxiety and suspicion often fill the information vacuum.

— The employees do not see a need for the change. Even if employees understand the reasons for change they may disagree with management's perspective and not agree that is needed.

— The employees are not involved in the planning. People support what they helped create. If employees do not believe they have enough input in planning change, resistance may increase.

— Communication regarding the reorganisation is poor. Even if the change affects only one other person, communication can be easily distorted.

— Key people in the organisation are not seen as really advocating the change. If employees believe their boss or other important individuals/groups don't support the change, acceptance is difficult to secure.

— The employees perceive a negative impact on their social relations. If employees view the change as adversely affecting the way they relate to people significant to them, acceptance is reduced.

— Key job characteristics are changed. Employees will be more resistant to the change if they believe it will decrease their autonomy, the level of challenge the job offers, the type of feedback they receive, or the degree of importance the organisation places on their jobs.

— The employees have been exposed to a long history of poorly-executed changes. If the employees believe that the organisation is involved in another ill-planned reorganisation, their enthusiasm will be greatly diminished.

— The employees fear failure. Change involves learning and learning usually involves mistakes; when people are not given the freedom to make mistakes while learning, they may be afraid and easily discouraged.

— The employees lack confidence in their capacity to implement the change, or in management's commitment to the training they need.

— Excessive pressure is involved. When employees are already feeling overworked, the additional pressure brought on by the change may create resistance.

— Employees perceive that organisational objectives of the change and their own personal goals are incompatible. Resistance is increased if employees believe the change will block or significantly restrict the achievement of their own personal ambitions.

Employee Development and Training

The challenges associated with the changing nature of work and the workplace environment are as real for the Berkeley campus as elsewhere. Rapid change requires a skilled, knowledgeable workforce with employees who are adaptive, flexible, and focused on the future.

As a manager, one of your key responsibilities is to develop your staff:

> "Encourage growth and career development of employees by coaching, and by helping employees achieve their personal goals at Berkeley and beyond [you can develop] human resources by providing adequate training... encouragement of staff development, and opportunities for growth."

The campus recognises that employee development requires a shared responsibility among the institution, you, and the employee. In this partnership: The institution

— ensures that policies and programmes facilitate the continuing development of staff You

— work with staff to:

— assess and provide feedback on their skills and interests

— select training and development activities that match their career development objectives and job needs

— use The Career Place site as a tool to tell employees about training and development opportunities on campus and to create an annual development plan

— stay informed of current policies and practices that support employee development

— follow up with employees after a learning activity to integrate new skills and knowledge into their responsibilities

The employee

— takes initiative to assess skills and interests and seek development activities that match needs

— works with you to identify training and development objectives

Most employee development and training programmes fall under the following categories:

— Management Development

— Career Development

— Basic Skills

— Professional Skills

— Technical Training

— Supervisory Skills

— Tuition Reduction

Your support of training and development creates a "win" for the employee and for your workplace. You will have:

— Employees with upgraded skills, working to their full potential and equipped to deal with the changing demands of the workplace

— Employees with higher morale, career satisfaction, creativity, and motivation

— Increased productivity and responsiveness in meeting departmental objectives

Management and leadership development

The management and leadership development process is flexible and continuous, linking an individual's development to the goals of the job and the organisation. Management development programmes on campus give you the opportunity to develop a broad base of skills and knowledge that can be applied to many jobs on campus. The overarching goal is a comprehensive curriculum for managers and supervisors to develop the necessary core competencies to become excellent leaders. The Employee Relations Unit also provides training for managers and supervisors, along with performance management tools. Expanding management core competencies will enable campus managers to keep pace with the demands of a changing organisation.

Management development activities can:

— Encourage growth and career development of employees

— Improve skills and knowledge that can be immediately applied at work

— Increase motivation and job satisfaction
— Create a network of colleagues for problem-solving and support
— Promote communication and planning throughout campus and department networks

How to support management development

— Model the behavior you are encouraging; don't neglect your own development.
— Discuss and create a development plan during the performance planning cycle.
— Endorse employees attending classes and activities that support development plans and goals.
— Discuss what the employee learned in classes and support integrating new ideas/methods.
— Provide timely behavioural feedback on performance and discuss ways to improve and develop further.
— Provide opportunities for your employees to develop through mentoring, cross-training, internships, campus staff organisations, professional associations, committee and task force assignments, skill assessment programmes and extension programmes.

Career development

Career development is the ongoing acquisition or refinement of skills and knowledge, including job mastery and professional development, coupled with career planning activities. Job mastery skills are those that are necessary to successfully perform one's job. Professional development skills are the skills and knowledge that go beyond the scope of the employee's job description, although they may indirectly improve job performance.

Since career development is an ongoing, dynamic process, employees may need encouragement and support in reviewing and reassessing their goals and activities. You are in a key position to provide valuable feedback and learning activities or resources. Formal training and classes away from the job are effective in providing new information, but adult learners also need to practice new skills. Therefore, you can contribute significantly to your staff member's career development by supporting career development activities within your department.

Your support for career development is important because:

— Current information about the organisation and future trends helps employees create more realistic career development goals

— Focus on skill development contributes to learning opportunities

— Opportunities for promotion and/or lateral moves contribute to the employee's career satisfaction

— A greater sense of responsibility for managing one's own career contributes to self-confidence

— Career planning and development clarifies the match between organisational and individual employee goals

— It's cost-effective to use your own staff talent to provide career development opportunities within your department

— Career development increases employee motivation and productivity

— Attention to career development helps you attract top staff and retain valued employees

— Supporting career development and growth of employees is mandated by the Philosophy of Human Resources Management

7

Interaction in the Workplace

When people think of diversity, they may think first of ethnicity and race, and then gender; however, diversity is much broader than that. Diversity is otherness or those human qualities that are different from our own and outside the groups to which we belong, yet present in other individuals and groups. Dimensions of diversity include, but are not limited to: age, ethnicity, ancestry, gender, physical abilities/qualities, race, sexual orientation, educational background, geographic location, income, marital status, military experience, religious beliefs, parental status, and work experience.

It's important to understand how these dimensions affect performance, motivation, success, and interactions with others. Institutional structures and practices that have presented barriers to some dimensions of diversity should be examined, challenged, and removed.

Managing Diversity

To address diversity issues, consider these questions: what policies, practices, and ways of thinking and within our organisational culture have differential impact on different groups? What organisational changes should be made to meet the needs of a diverse workforce as well as to maximise the potential of all workers, so that Berkeley can be well positioned for the demands of the 21st century?

Most people believe in the golden rule: treat others as you want to be treated. The implicit assumption is that how you want to be treated is how others want to be treated. But when you look at this proverb through a diversity perspective, you begin to ask the question: what does respect look like; does it look the same for everyone? Does it mean saying hello in the morning, or leaving someone alone, or making eye contact when you speak?

It depends on the individual. We may share similar values, such as respect or need for recognition, but how we show those values through behaviour may be different for different cultures. How do we know what different cultures need? Perhaps instead of using the golden rule, we could use the platinum rule which states: "treat others as they want to be treated."

Managers have a key role in transforming the organisational culture so that it more closely reflects the values of the diverse workforce. Some of the skills needed are:

— an understanding and acceptance of managing diversity concepts

— recognition that diversity is threaded through every aspect of management

— self-awareness, in terms of understanding your own culture, identity, biases, prejudices, and stereotypes

— willingness to challenge and change institutional practices that present barriers to different groups

It's natural to want a cookbook approach to diversity issues so that one knows exactly what to do. Unfortunately, given the many dimensions of diversity, there is no easy recipe to follow. Advice and strategies given for one situation may not work given the same situation in another context.

Managing diversity means acknowledging people's differences and recognising these differences as valuable; it enhances good management practices by preventing discrimination and promoting inclusiveness. Good management alone will not necessarily help you work effectively with a diverse workforce. It is often difficult to see what part diversity plays in a specific area of management.

Issues

— How do you make the job sound appealing to different types of workers, such as people with disabilities?

— How can recruitment be effectively targeted to underutilised groups?

— How do you overcome cultural bias in the interviewing process, questions, and your response?

Strategies

— Specify the need for skills to work effectively in a diverse environment in the job, for example: "demonstrated ability to work effectively in a diverse work environment."

— Make sure that good faith efforts are made to recruit a diverse applicant pool, particularly underutilised minorities and women.

— Focus on the job requirements in the interview, and assess experience but also consider

— transferable skills and demonstrated competencies, such as analytical, organisational, communication, coordination. Prior experience has not necessarily mean effectiveness or success on the job.

— Use a panel interview format. Ensure that the committee is diverse, unit affiliation, job classification, length of service, variety of life experiences, etc. to represent different perspectives and to eliminate bias from the selection process. Run questions and process by them to ensure there is no unintentional cultural or institutional bias.

— Ensure that appropriate accommodations are made for disabled applicants.

— Know your own cultural biases. What stereotypes do you have of people from different groups and how well they may perform on the job? What communication styles do you prefer? Sometimes what we consider to be appropriate or desirable qualities in a candidate may reflect more about our personal preferences than about the skills needed to perform the job.

Fair vs. Same Treatment

Many people think that "fairness" means "treating everyone the same." How well does treating everyone the same work for a diverse staff? For example, when employees have limited English language skills or reading proficiency, even though that limit might not affect their ability to do their jobs, transmitting important information through complicated memos might not be an effective way of communicating with them. While distributing such memos to all staff is "treating everyone the same," this approach may not communicate essential information to everyone.

A staff member who missed out on essential information might feel that the communication process was "unfair." A process that takes account of the diverse levels of English language and reading proficiency among the staff might include taking extra time to be sure that information in an important memorandum is understood. Such efforts on the part of supervisors and managers should be supported and rewarded as good management practices for working with a diverse staff.

Managing Diversity from Affirmative Action

Managing diversity focuses on maximising the ability of all employees to contribute to organisational goals. Affirmative action focuses on specific groups because of historical discrimination, such as people of color and women. Affirmative action emphasizes legal necessity and social responsibility; managing diversity emphasizes business necessity. In short, while managing diversity is also concerned with underrepresentation of women and people of color in the workforce, it is much more inclusive and acknowledges that diversity must work for everyone.

Ignoring diversity issues costs time, money, and efficiency. Some of the consequences can include unhealthy tensions between people of differing gender, race, ethnicity, age, abilities, etc.; loss of productivity because of increased conflict; inability to attract and retain talented people of all kinds; complaints and legal actions; and inability to retain women and people of color, resulting in lost investments in recruitment and training.

Communication

Communication is an important part of your job one that is often taken for granted. When you think about it, almost everything you do calls for good communications. When you hire a new employee, good communication skills help you pick the right person and make sure the person you hire knows what the job involves. When you're training, coaching, or evaluating an employee, you need to be clear about your expectations and sensitive in dealing with problem areas. When conflicts arise, you'll need your communication skills to resolve the issues without creating more.

When the department is going through changes or a reorganisation, you'll need special communication skills to get feedback and ideas from your staff and to give them news that's sometimes not pleasant, while keeping them motivated. Honest communication is one of the key ingredients in managing change as well as managing people.

Good communication can help you:

— Improve relationships and teamwork

— Improve performance and productivity

— Foster an open, creative environment

— Solve problems effectively

Becoming a better communicator

Your responsibility as a supervisor is to communicate clearly and concisely to all employees and create an environment conducive to openness for others. As the staff become more diverse, you may have to take extra time and effort to communicate to all staff members. To become a better communicator:

— Create an open communication environment in your unit. Encourage employees to talk about work issues; listen carefully and respond to questions or concerns with actions or answers. If an issue is outside your authority, pass it along to the appropriate person; then be sure to follow up.

— Conduct regular staff meetings. Tell your staff about decisions that may affect them or the work they do and the reasons for those decisions. Use staff meetings to encourage feedback, generate ideas, solve problems, and gain support.

— Set up individual meetings. Set some time aside periodically to meet one-on-one with employees. Group staff meetings are important; however, meeting separately with your employees shows concern about their individual work issues.

Effective listening

An important ingredient that runs through all good communication is listening. Listening is a skill that can be practiced and learned. Your goal as a listener is to fully understand your employee's experience and point of view. Give the employee a chance to talk for a while before you say anything.

— Use nonverbal communication. Be aware of what you communicate with your body; your posture and expressions can convey your attitudes toward a speaker even before you say one word. Use body language to show the speaker that you are engaged in the conversation and open to hearing.

— Recognise your own prejudices. Be aware of your own feelings toward the speaker. If you are unsure about what the speaker means, ask for clarification instead of making assumptions.

— Listen to understand the underlying feelings. Use your heart as well as your mind to understand the speaker. Notice how something is said as well as the actual words used.

— Don't interrupt: Be sure you think carefully before you speak. As a listener, your job is to help the speaker express himself.

— Don't judge the person: A speaker who feels you are making judgments will feel defensive. Avoid making judgments and instead try to empathise and understand the speaker's perspective.

— Do not give advice: Keep in mind that the best resolutions are those that people arrive at themselves, not what someone else tells them to do. If you feel it is appropriate, and only after you have encouraged the person to talk, offer some ideas and discuss them.

Responding

After you have listened and really heard, respond by conveying your interest and respect:

— Empathize: Put yourself in the other person's shoes and try to understand.

— Validate: Acknowledge that the person's feelings are valid. This is a very powerful tool because you are recognizing the person's right to feel that way, regardless of whether you would feel the same way.

— Restate what the other person has said: this allows you to make sure you understand the feelings and shows you are listening. Point out the good things the person has done or tried to do.

— Clarify: Ask questions to get more information about the problem.

— Summarise: Paraphrase the main points you have heard so that you can make sure you understand all the issues.

Team Building

Team building is an ongoing process that helps a work group evolve into a cohesive unit. The team members not only share expectations for accomplishing group tasks, but trust and support one another and respect one another's individual differences. Your role as a team builder is to lead your team toward cohesiveness and productivity. A team takes on a life of its own and you have to regularly nurture and maintain it, just as you do for individual employees. Your Employee Relations Specialist can advise and help you.

With good team-building skills, you can unite employees around a common goal and generate greater productivity. Without them, you limit yourself and the staff to the effort each individual can make alone.

Team building can lead to:

— Good communications with participants as team members and individuals
— Increased department productivity and creativity
— Team members motivated to achieve goals
— A climate of cooperation and collaborative problem-solving
— Higher levels of job satisfaction and commitment
— Higher levels of trust and support
— Diverse co-workers working well together
— Clear work objectives
— Better operating policies and procedures

Symptoms that Signal a Need for Team Building

— Decreased productivity
— Conflicts or hostility among staff members
— Confusion about assignments, missed signals, and unclear relationships
— Decisions misunderstood or not carried through properly
— Apathy and lack of involvement

— Lack of initiation, imagination, innovation; routine actions taken for solving complex problems
— Complaints of discrimination or favouritism
— Ineffective staff meetings, low participation, minimally effective decisions
— Negative reactions to the manager
— Complaints about quality of service

Steps to Building an Effective Team

The first rule of team building is an obvious one: to lead a team effectively, you must first establish your leadership with each team member. Remember that the most effective team leaders build their relationships of trust and loyalty, rather than fear or the power of their positions.

— Consider each employee's ideas as valuable. Remember that there is no such thing as a stupid idea.
— Be aware of employees' unspoken feelings. Set an example to team members by being open with employees and sensitive to their moods and feelings.
— Act as a harmonizing influence. Look for chances to mediate and resolve minor disputes; point continually toward the team's higher goals.
— Be clear when communicating. Be careful to clarify directives.
— Encourage trust and cooperation among employees on your team. Remember that the relationships team members establish among themselves are every bit as important as those you establish with them. As the team begins to take shape, pay close attention to the ways in which team members work together and take steps to improve communication, cooperation, trust, and respect in those relationships.

— Encourage team members to share information. Emphasize the importance of each team member's contribution and demonstrate how all of their jobs operate together to move the entire team closer to its goal.

— Delegate problem-solving tasks to the team. Let the team work on creative solutions together.

— Facilitate communication. Remember that communication is the single most important factor in successful teamwork. Facilitating communication does not mean holding meetings all the time. Instead it means setting an example by remaining open to suggestions and concerns, by asking questions and offering help, and by doing everything you can to avoid confusion in your own communication.

— Establish team values and goals; evaluate team performance. Be sure to talk with members about the progress they are making toward established goals so that employees get a sense both of their success and of the challenges that lie ahead. Address teamwork in performance standards. Discuss with your team:

— What do we really care about in performing our job?

— What does the word success mean to this team?

— What actions can we take to live up to our stated values?

— Make sure that you have a clear idea of what you need to accomplish; that you know what your standards for success are going to be; that you have established clear time frames; and that team members understand their responsibilities.

— Use consensus. Set objectives, solve problems, and plan for action. While it takes much longer to establish consensus, this method ultimately provides better decisions and greater productivity because it secures every employee's commitment to all phases of the work.

— Set ground rules for the team. These are the norms that you and the team establish to ensure efficiency and success. They can be simple directives (Team members are to be punctual for meetings) or general guidelines (Every team member has the right to offer ideas and suggestions), but you should make sure that the team creates these ground rules by consensus and commits to them, both as a group and as individuals.

— Establish a method for arriving at a consensus. You may want to conduct open debate about the pros and cons of proposals, or establish research committees to investigate issues and deliver reports.

— Encourage listening and brainstorming. As supervisor, your first priority in creating consensus is to stimulate debate. Remember that employees are often afraid to disagree with one another and that this fear can lead your team to make mediocre decisions. When you encourage debate you inspire creativity and that's how you'll spur your team on to better results.

— Establish the parameters of consensus-building sessions. Be sensitive to the frustration that can mount when the team is not achieving consensus. At the outset of your meeting, establish time limits, and work with the team to achieve consensus within those parameters. Watch out for false consensus; if an agreement is struck too quickly, be careful to probe individual team members to discover their real feelings about the proposed solution.

Managing Conflict

Most conflicts, neither party is right or wrong; instead,

different perceptions collide to create disagreement. Conflict is natural and it's up to you to respond to conflict situations quickly and professionally. Conflict can be very positive; if you deal with it openly, you can strengthen your work unit by correcting problems. Conflicting views give you a chance to learn more about yourself, explore views of others, and develop productive relationships. Clear and open communication is the cornerstone of successful conflict resolution.

By managing conflicts skilfully, you can:

— Gain cooperation from team members

— Improve performance and productivity

— Reduce stress and preserve integrity

— Solve problems as quickly as possible

— Improve relationships and teamwork

— Enhance creativity

— Increase staff morale

Resolving Conflict Situations

To manage conflict effectively you must be a skilled communicator. That includes creating an open communication environment in your unit by encouraging employees to talk about work issues. Listening to employee concerns will foster an open environment. Make sure you really understand what employees are saying by asking questions and focusing on their perception of the problem.

Whether you have two employees who are fighting for the desk next to the window or one employee who wants the heat on and another who doesn't, your immediate response to conflict situations is essential. Here are some tips you can use when faced with employees who can't resolve their own conflicts.

— Acknowledge that a difficult situation exists. Honesty and clear communication play an important role in the resolution process. Acquaint yourself with what's happening and be open about the problem.

— Let individuals express their feelings. Some feelings of anger and/or hurt usually accompany conflict situations. Before any kind of problem-solving can take place, these emotions should be expressed and acknowledged.

— Define the problem. What is the stated problem? What is the negative impact on the work or relationships? Are differing personality styles part of the problem? Meet with employees separately at first and question them about the situation.

— Determine underlying need. The goal of conflict resolution is not to decide which person is right or wrong; the goal is to reach a solution that everyone can live with. Looking first for needs, rather than solutions, is a powerful tool for generating win/win options. To discover needs, you must try to find out why people want the solutions they initially proposed. Once you understand the advantages their solutions have for them, you have discovered their needs.

— Find common areas of agreement, no matter how small:

— Agree on the problem

— Agree on the procedure to follow

— Agree on worst fears

— Agree on some small change to give an experience of success

— Find solutions to satisfy needs:

— Problem-solve by generating multiple alternatives

— Determine which actions will be taken

— Make sure involved parties buy into actions. (Total silence may be a sign of passive resistance.) Be sure you get real agreement from everyone.

— Determine follow-up you will take to monitor actions. You may want to schedule a follow-up meeting in about two weeks to determine how the parties are doing.

— Determine what you'll do if the conflict goes unresolved. If the conflict is causing a disruption in the department and it remains unresolved, you may need to explore other avenues. An outside facilitator (such as the Staff Ombuds Office) may be able to offer other insights on solving the problem. In some cases the conflict becomes a performance issue, and may become a topic for coaching sessions, performance appraisals, or disciplinary action.

Dealing With Anger

When you meet with someone who is angry, you can use the tools of effective listening to help defuse this anger. Nevertheless, when anger is directed at you, it is much more difficult to respond definitively, because your own emotions are usually involved.

To effectively defuse anger, keep in mind the needs of the angry speaker:

— To vent. An angry person needs to let off steam and release the anger that may have been brewing for a long time use your communication skills to allow the person to do this.

— To get the listener's attention. An angry person wants to know that you are paying attention use your body language to show this.

— To be heard. An angry person wants someone to listen to her point of view acknowledge the feelings you hear so that the speaker knows you appreciate how angry she is.

— To be understood. An angry person wants someone to appreciate how she feels try to empathize with her experience so that she feels you understand the situation, and acknowledge her right to feel the way she does.

When you're listening to an angry person:

— *Be attentive and patient.* Keep in mind that she will become less angry as you let her express herself.

— *Be sincere.* Empathy and validation must be both honest and genuine.

— *Be calm.* Try to remove your own emotions from the discussion. Remember that an angry person may say inflammatory things in the heat of the moment, but you do not have to react angrily.

Sexual Harassment

You have the leadership role in recognising that sexual harassment does exist in the work environment, and you must make conscientious efforts to eradicate it. You have the responsibility to participate in the creation of a campus environment free from sexual harassment and in the resolving complaints within your respective jurisdictions.

Preventing sexual harassment

— Monitor the working environment to make sure behavior that may be perceived as sexual harassment stops.

— Raise the subject in staff meetings and express strong disapproval.

— Communicate and distribute the campus harassment policy and complaint resolution procedures to all employees.
— Post the official sexual harassment policy and brochure in your department.
— Know and understand what types of behavior may constitute sexual harassment.

When you receive a Complaint

— Take every complaint seriously, no matter how frivolous it may seem.
— Contact the Title IX Compliance Officer for advice.
— Investigate every complaint immediately and thoroughly.
— Remain objective and maintain a professional approach.
— Avoid making judgments without all the facts.
— Talk to the alleged harasser.
— Interview anyone who might have witnessed the conduct.
— Keep the process as confidential as possible.
— Document every step of the investigation in detail.
— Take appropriate remedial and/or corrective action.
— Advise the complaining employee that appropriate action has been taken and that any future incidents should be reported immediately.

Health and Safety

The campus is committed to providing a safe and healthy work environment for its faculty and staff. You play a special role in making sure this commitment is carried out. You are the front-line expert who best knows your workplace, the employees, and the demands they face. Therefore, you play a critical role in identifying possible health and safety problems in your workplace.

You are a key link to campus resources which have been set up to handle workplace health and safety issues. While you are not expected to know everything about workplace health and safety issues, you should know when and how to use campus resources.

You are a role model and motivator for employees in your department. The importance you place on workplace health and safety issues is conveyed to them by your actions as well as your words.

Your goals in health and safety are to:

— Foster a safe and healthy work environment by providing training and proper equipment and by modeling and rewarding safe and healthy work practices

— Prevent injuries and illnesses to reduce the human and financial costs associated with Workers' Compensation, disability, and health care

— Recruit and retain the best employees by being a supervisor who cares about the well-being of faculty and staff

Occupational Health Clinic

The Occupational Health Clinic provides these direct treatment and preventive services to employees:

— Consultation on campus health problems, including environmental, occupational, ergonomic, and general health concerns

— Urgent medical care and ongoing treatment for work-related injuries and illnesses at no charge to the employee

— Periodic medical screening and immunisation programmes for employees who are exposed to potential health risks on the job

— Medical consultations for individuals with medical concerns related to laboratory and other exposures

— Specific screening and training programmes on occupational health issues, such as hearing conservation

— Learn about occupational health issues relevant to your workplace.

— Assess potential health risks at your workplace regularly and act promptly to correct hazardous situations in accordance with your department's Injury and Illness Prevention Programme

— Discuss workplace health and safety issues at staff meetings.

— Provide health and safety training for your department.

— Ensure that employees participate in medical screening and immunisation programmes applicable to their jobs.

— Assure employees get appropriate medical treatment for work-related injuries and illnesses.

Consult with the Occupational Health Clinic in special circumstances, such as:

— If an employee's medical problem may be causing a health or safety hazard

— If there may be a need for medical evaluation of a problem that is impairing job performance

Disability Management

Disabilities can be work-related, or they may occur away

from work or be congenital. Disability management refers to the steps you take to assure that an employee can return to work as soon as possible. An important piece of case management is preventing work-related injuries by identifying and correcting potential hazards, from chemicals to poorly designed workstations.

If a work-related injury does occur, handling the case appropriately can encourage a prompt recovery, save money, decrease the chance of delayed benefits, and allow the unit to continue to get the work done. For non-work-related disabilities, it's also important to complete the forms sent to the department by the Benefits Unit on time and to pay the employee's sick leave correctly.

Issues for managers include:

— Taking steps to prevent injuries from occurring at work

— Assuring that an employee receives medical treatment if an injury occurs

— Knowing how the injured employee is doing and whether the department can help with any problems or concerns

— Facilitating the payment of benefits and salary

— Planning ahead to allow for a longer-than-expected period of disability

— Providing modified work when available

For effective disability management:

— Ensure that the work environment is safe, both physically and psychologically

— Make sure that employees get medical attention if injuries do occur

— Manage disability cases effectively to make sure that the work is done in an employee's absence

- — Determine and document eligibility for federal or state family and medical leave in accordance with policy or contract
- — Separate disability issues from performance issues
- — Stay in touch with the employee to keep her informed of events in the office, assure that her salary and benefits are being correctly handled, and stay up to date on her recovery and expected return-to-work date
- — Help the employee make a successful return to work through accommodation as needed and reorientation into the office

Workers' Compensation

Workers' Compensation is a state-mandated benefit that requires all employers to pay for approved expenses resulting from a work-related injury or illness. This includes, for example, the employee who slips and falls on the job resulting in a broken ankle; the employee who, over the course of years, injures her back from repeated lifting; and the employee who develops a rash from exposure to chemicals. This benefit is designed to be no-fault (blame is not assigned).

- — Take steps to prevent injuries from occurring.
- — Assure employee receives medical treatment. In an emergency, call the police department.
- — Keep in touch. When the employee is off work, maintain regular contact. This will help the employee keep up with any departmental changes and let her know that she is a valued member of the unit, and will help you to know how the employee is doing and effectively cover her workload.
- — Review and comment on a job description form. If the employee loses 90 or more calendar days of work following the injury, you will be asked to review a

specialised job description form. This two-page form is completed by the employee and counselor and involves a description of the physical demands of the job for orthopedic injuries and mental demands for emotional injury or stress claims. Your comments will be added to the form.

— Review medical and vocational information for possible accommodation to a modified or alternative position for employees with permanent work restrictions.

Payments to the Employee

When the employee is off work for a compensable injury, she will be receiving temporary disability payments directly from ORS; these payments can be used in conjunction with her sick and, if chosen, vacation leave. Thus an employee who has an injury and has a great amount of sick leave might stay on full pay status for an extended period. Once the employee's sick and/or vacation leave is exhausted, the employee is entitled to Extended Sick Leave (ESL) for up to six months, as long as she remains disabled. The difference between the Workers' Compensation benefit and 80% salary paid during ESL is made up from departmental funds.

To be eligible for the 80% ESL benefit, an employee must first exhaust her own sick leave. Vacation leave may also be used, but this is not required to be eligible for ESL. If the employee chooses to keep the Workers' Compensation checks and not use sick leave, she will not be on pay status and will be responsible for paying for all of her own health benefits.

Because the employee is on pay status and receiving salary checks, any checks from ORS that the employee cashes will be deducted from a future paycheck. This sometimes occurs after the employee has returned to work.

Employee Benefits

While on pay status, the employee's benefits continue as normal. Sick/vacation leave is also accrued at the normal rate and service credit is accrued according to the percentage of salary received (i.e., on 80% pay, 80% service credit is accrued). When the employee goes onto leave without pay status, she continues to accrue sick/vacation leave (to be credited only if she returns to work) and has her medical insurance premiums paid as long as she is receiving temporary disability payments.

Non-Work-Related Injuries

The steps for non-work-related injuries are not as detailed as those for work-related injuries, but they are just as important. If you have an employee who gets injured off the job follow these guidelines:

— Get written verification from the doctor stating the length of time the employee will be out of work.

— Refer the employee to the Benefits Unit to apply for disability if the employee's disability extends longer than the available sick and vacation leaves.

— After exhausting up to thirty calendar days of accrued sick leave (about 22 working days), if your employee wants to, you can authorise the use of vacation time, particularly if the waiting period for the disability benefit is longer than the number of sick days available. The employee must be on leave without pay to get disability benefits.

— Fill out the Department Time Verification form, which will be sent to the department by the Benefits Unit once the employee applies for disability under group insurance. This form details the last day worked, sick leave and vacation leave used, and when the employee went on leave without pay. This information is reported to the disability insurance carrier and is needed before a claim can be opened. Disability benefits begin when the claim is approved and the employee is on leave without pay.

— Change the employee's record in HRMS to indicate leave without pay when the employee has exhausted sick leave and/or any vacation days.

— Keep in touch with the employee during her absence.

Vocational Rehabilitation

The rehabilitation programmemes help disabled faculty and staff members (for work-related and non-work-related injuries) stay on the job through accommodation or find other work consistent with their medical limitations.

Services for employees can include:

— Vocational assessment

— Job-seeking skills

— Interview and resume preparation

— Job search

For supervisors, the Vocational Rehabilitation Counselors:

— Help get medical clarification of an employee's restrictions

— Perform medical separation reviews

— Provide resource information about adaptive equipment and services and accommodation

Supervisors supervise an employee with a disability or you may be contacted by a counselor to consider interviewing/ hiring an employee with a disability from another department. Specific areas where you would have a role include:

Search for alternative work. If an employee is medically unable to return to her previously held position, you will be asked by a counselor to review the possibility of transferring her to an open position in the unit for which she is qualified and which she is medically able to perform. If there are restrictions, you are responsible for determining whether reasonable accommodation is possible. If accommodation is not possible you would work with your Employee Relations Specialist to determine whether it is appropriate to request a medical separation.

Job analysis. A counselor would meet with you at the employee's work site to discuss the demands of the position. The analysis is then reviewed by the employee. Comments are discussed again with you so that any disagreements can be clarified.

Return to Work

In preparing for an employee's return to work following a period of disability, you should: Request in writing, about two weeks prior to the expected return date, that the employee provide either:

— a full release slip from the doctor OR
— a slip from the doctor indicating that the disability is being extended to a specific date OR
— a slip from the doctor stating that the employee will have restrictions on her return to work (this note should indicate the nature and duration of the restrictions)

If the employee returns to work part-time for medical reasons related to the medical leave or if the employee may lose time for doctor's appointments or therapy, she may be eligible for supplemental benefits from either ORS for work-related injuries or Liberty Mutual (UC's disability carrier) for non-work-related injuries. The following steps will ensure that the employee is properly compensated:

For work-related injuries, report the return to work to a Workers' Compensation Benefits Assistant and indicate whether the return is to less than full time. If the schedule is to be consistent (i.e., four hours per day for three weeks), ORS will calculate benefits on a wage loss basis.

If the employee is returning from a non-work-related injury or illness, she may be eligible for supplemental benefits from Liberty Mutual. For example, if an employee returns half-time due to a medical restriction, Liberty Mutual may make up the difference to the 70% maximum benefit level. This benefit is called Rehabilitation Status and should be requested in writing to Liberty Mutual. Contact the Benefits Unit for more information.

Modified Work Programme

The Hotel began a campus-wide modified work programme in January 1991, following a successful pilot programme. Providing modified work has several advantages:

— It is an effective way for employees to return to full duty. It is cost-effective for both the department-which pays for work vs. sick leave and the campus in overall claims cost

— It is psychologically advantageous to the employee

— In this programme, restrictions on an employee's work may be accommodated for up to 60 days with a possible 60-day extension.

The employee may be accommodated in the previously held position (through eliminating tasks outside the restrictions, performing tasks in a different manner, or reducting time) or assigned duties other than her usual responsibilities. The employee will be expected to work a productive schedule for the time she is assigned. The salary remains the same (even if in a lower position) or is increased (if in a higher level position).

Role of Employees

— Obtain a medical slip from the employee that outlines the restrictions and their duration. If you can't evaluate for reasonable accommodation with the information provided or if no length of time is given for the restrictions, contact the Vocational Rehabilitation Counselor assigned to your control unit. The counselor will contact the doctor directly for further information. If the employee was seen by a physician at Occupational Health Service, you may call directly for information. Determine whether the restrictions can be accommodated in either the previously held or an alternative position.

— Contact the employee with your assessment and, if you can accommodate, set a return-to-work date. If the restrictions involve a part-time schedule, set a work schedule. Always acknowledge receipt of the restrictions in writing and outline in writing what accommodations you are able to make. For example, if the accommodation involves a change in duties, outline what the employee will be doing. If the duration of the restrictions is two months and you can only accommodate for one month, specify that in the letter and indicate that you will re-evaluate the possibility of an extension at the end of that month.

— Send a copy of the letter to the Vocational Rehabilitation Counselor so that the modified work can be documented and included in annual programme evaluations.

— Request that the employee provide further medical documentation at the end of the modified work period, indicating that she is released to full duty or that the restrictions need to be continued and/or modified.

— The department can request an independent medical opinion. The need for this should be evaluated on a case-by-case basis. The department is responsible for paying the cost of the evaluation and report.

Benefits

Every department has a Department Benefits Counselor (DBC) who has current plan literature, eligibility rules, and enrollment procedures. The DBC provides front-line benefits information to new and continuing employees, helps employees through the enrollment process, and assists management throughout the employment life cycle in communicating benefits options. While it is not appropriate for DBCs to make decisions about benefits or take benefits action on behalf of employees, they can help by referring employees to the resources that are available. The DBCs work closely with Human Resources Benefits staff, who provide training and information with regular communications through e-mail and the Human Resources Web site.

As a manager or supervisor, you are not expected to know all the details pertaining to benefits plans. However, you should:

— Understand the scope of benefit programmes

— Be aware of eligibility issues when structuring new appointments or changing existing appointments

— Encourage employees to use telephone and web-based systems for getting information and taking benefits actions

— Know which events in the employee's life cycle trigger changes in eligibility

— Be sure that employees know about all benefits options available to them and that they are enrolled by applicable deadlines

— Assure that when eligibility or coverage ends, the employee has access to information on possible options

— Advise employees to contact the Benefits Unit to apply for benefits (such as disability and retirement) as soon as you become aware of special situations

— Encourage employees to consider their options when new benefits are introduced, or during special periods of eligibility such as the annual Open Enrollment Period

8

Hiring and Supervising Employees

Individuals looking for work (supply) and the jobs available in a given area (demand) make up the labour market. When demand for workers is high and the supply of qualified workers is low, properly staffing a hospitality operation becomes very challenging for management.

Other factors have an important impact on the labour market as well. When you need to fill jobs, you look for individuals with certain knowledge levels, skills, abilities, and attitudes. So, the location of your operation will certainly influence factors such as educational levels, average age of population, personality types, unemployment rates, and so forth.

In addition, keep in mind you are competing with other restaurants, hotels, bars, caterers, and even hospitals, banks, nursing homes, and large retail organisations such as Wal-Mart for the same prospective employees, so the recruiting strategies of your competitors as well as their ability to perhaps offer higher wages and/or better fringe benefits will have a lot to do with your hiring success. Remember, too, that many hospitality graduates find themselves managing or even owning small operations without the means or the budget to employ a full-blown, professionally staffed human resources department to handle the day-to-day hiring of employees. In fact, as the owner, manager, or supervisor at a smaller operation, you are the human resources department.

Hospitality Industry Jobs

While much progress has been made over the years to improve the image of hospitality industry careers, many prospective employees still do not see hotel and restaurant jobs as a viable career choice. This is likely due to an abundance of low-wage, entry-level, part-time jobs. Many of these back-of-house jobs require hard work either standing in a hot kitchen or hotel laundry area, cleaning floors and scrubbing toilets, or loading and unloading dishes and pots and pans into a steaming, noisy dishwasher. Where's the glamour in that?

More often than not, front-of-house positions, too, seem less glamorous when coupled with the demands of carrying heavy trays of food or constantly dealing with demanding guests and clientele. It is no surprise that the duller and more demanding jobs are more difficult to fill, but the good news is that there are people with no experience and no skills who are willing to take these jobs and who, with proper incentives and training, often become valuable, long-term employees.

The hospitality industry has become so competitive that if customers and employees are dissatisfied, they will go elsewhere. We want to be able to trust the people we do business with, but life has become more difficult and expensive, and ethical shortcuts have become the norm. The following 10 Ethical Principles for Hospitality Managers were adopted from Josephson Institute of Ethics' "Core Ethical Principles." They have served as the basis of ethics research coming out of Isbell Hospitality Ethics for the past 15 years. Adherence to these principles will result in the best consequences for all parties involved.

— *Honesty:* Hospitality managers are honest and truthful. They do not mislead or deceive others by misrepresentations.

— *Integrity*: Hospitality managers demonstrate the courage of their convictions by doing what they know is right even when there is pressure to do otherwise.

— *Trustworthiness*: Hospitality managers are trustworthy and candid in supplying information and in correcting misapprehensions of fact. They do not create justifications for escaping their promises and commitments.

— *Loyalty*: Hospitality managers demonstrate loyalty to their companies in devotion to duty and loyalty to colleagues by friendship in adversity. They avoid conflicts of interest; do not use or disclose confidential information; and, should they accept other employment, they respect the proprietary information of their former employer.

— *Fairness*: Hospitality managers are fair and equitable in all dealings; they neither arbitrarily abuse power nor take undue advantage of another's mistakes or difficulties. They treat all individuals with equality, with tolerance and acceptance of diversity, and with an open mind.

— *Concern and respect for others*: Hospitality managers are concerned, respectful, compassionate, and kind. They are sensitive to the personal concerns of their colleagues and live the Golden Rule. They respect the rights and interests of all those who have a stake in their decisions.

— *Commitment to excellence*: Hospitality managers pursue excellence in performing their duties and are willing to put more into their job than they can get out of it.

— *Leadership*: Hospitality managers are conscious of the responsibility and opportunities of their position of leadership. They realise that the best way to instill ethical principles and ethical awareness in their organisations is by example. They walk their talk!

— *Reputation and morale*: Hospitality managers seek to protect and build the company's reputation and the morale of its employees by engaging in conduct that builds respect. They also take whatever actions are necessary to correct or prevent inappropriate conduct of others.

— *Accountability*: Hospitality managers are personally accountable for the ethical quality of their decisions, as well as those of their subordinates.

Demographic Changes

Demographic changes will also pose new challenges. Demographics are statistics that include such things as a target group's age, race, sex, income, and educational levels. According to the U.S. Bureau of Labour Statistics, the composition of the labour force is expected to change as general population demographics change. For example, in 2010, the baby boom generation will be ages 45 to 64, and this age group will account for a 5 percent larger share of the labour force than it does currently. And even though the 16- to 24-year-old age group is expected to now grow more rapidly than the overall labour force for the first time in 25 years, the median age of the labour force will continue to rise .

Because of high net immigration and higher-than-average birth rates, the Asian and Other and Hispanic labour force groups are projected to increase faster than other groups. The Asian and Other group is expected to grow 44 percent and thereby increase its share of the labour force from 5 to 6 percent. The Hispanic labour force will grow by 36 percent, increasing its share from 11 percent to 13 percent of the total workforce. The Black labour force is expected to grow by 21 percent, more than twice as fast as the White labour force (9 percent).

According to the Bureau of Labour Statistics, other indirect changes will emerge as a result of the country's changing demographics. The likelihood of working side by side with people who are different-in culture, gender, age, and many other ways-will increase, as well as the challenges that hospitality industry managers will face in attracting and retaining a quality workforce with so much competition out there.

Traditional Workers

With fewer traditional workers to fill the growing demand for hospitality industry employees, many organisations have made a concerted effort to recruit what is often referred to as a nontraditional employee. Table 1 lists some typical characteristics of a nontraditional worker.

Table 1. Labour sources for nontraditional hospitality industry workers.

Nontraditional workers in the hospitality industry might include the following:
— Retirees hoping to supplement retirement income with part-time, flexible hours
— Recent immigrants who may or may not speak English
— Disabled individuals
— Displaced homemakers
— Career changers

In almost every community, large and small, one needs only to go out to dinner on a busy Friday or Saturday night to witness first-hand the explosive growth of our nation's restaurant industry. If you are unfortunate enough to show up without a reservation, the wait can be in excess of an hour or more in some communities.

Household incomes have risen dramatically in the past decade, which is good news for the restaurant industry. When people have more money to spend, they are more likely to dine out and spend it in restaurants. For many people, the restaurant table is beginning to replace the dinner table at home. Consider these mind-boggling statistics from the National Restaurant Association's 2005 Restaurant Industry Forecast:

— Restaurant industry sales reached a record $453.5 billion in 2004-an increase of 5.5 percent from 2003.

— Restaurants will provide more than 70 billion meal and snack occasions in 2005.

— The typical adult purchased a meal or snack from a restaurant 5.3 times a week, on average, in 2004.

— By the year 2015, restaurant industry employment will reach 14.0 million.

— Roughly 900,000 locations offer food service nationwide-up a strong 83 percent from 1972.

Many restaurants and most lodging properties rely heavily on tourism. Higher-end full-service restaurants estimate that up to 30 percent of their sales are driven by travellers and visitors. When people do have expendable income, they often choose to dine out. They may be dining out for special occasions such as birthdays or anniversaries, or they may simply be enjoying the company of friends and families. Customers who visit lodging and food service establishments today are very different from those of 50 years ago. At that time, dining out was a luxury; now, it's commonplace. Today's consumer is extremely savvy when it comes to food, service, restaurant or hotel ambience, and travel in general.

When many of today's baby boomers were growing up in the late 1950s and 1960s, going out to eat with the family was a rare, special treat, often reserved for Sunday dinner. Young people today may have eaten more restaurant meals in their lifetime than they have eaten in their homes! This familiarity with the restaurant and food service industry has created a generation of diners who have sophisticated tastes with respect to the quality of food and service they expect to receive when dining out. Some experts attribute this to cable TV shows such as those found on the Food Network and the explosion in the popularity of celebrity TV chefs, such as Emeril Lagasse.

Whatever the reason, the bar has been raised considerably, so it is more important than ever that managers and supervisors in the hospitality industry are able to attract the right applicant for the right job; provide that new employee with valuable, ongoing training; and then offer the kind of work environment in which the new employee can self-motivate and become a valuable member of the team.

Motivations and Expectations

Guests and customers visit various hospitality operations today with very distinct motivations, needs, and expectations (MNEs). Your ability to not only meet but actually exceed your guests' MNEs will play a large role in determining your operation's success or failure. The most successful hospitality enterprises understand this concept quite well, and those operations also understand that the very best way to meet and exceed customer MNEs is to have a well-trained, dynamic, and motivated staff.

Quality management and leadership is also of the utmost importance; once you have made that all-important hiring decision, the truly hard work has not yet even begun-that is, the training you must provide and management practices that you must consistently adhere to in order to provide the kind of work environment in which your employees can self-motivate and provide high-quality products and services to your valued guests. There are probably as many reasons for dining out as there are locations to do so. Of course, when we're hungry, we eat, but surprisingly, the simple need for one to put food in one's belly is not a primary motivator for dining out in many cases.

Hospitality businesses that understand their customers' MNEs and that regularly meet and exceed them are well on their way to success. Each restaurant to fail miserably in meeting its customers' MNEs. Keep in mind that travellers who require overnight lodging come armed with their own special set of MNEs. These concepts can just as easily be applied to any segment of the large and diverse hospitality industry.

Clearly, what motivates us to seek a dining experience as well as what we need and expect to get out of that experience is not always a simple matter. Producing quality products and providing top-notch service requires motivated, well-trained employees. Hospitality managers who understand this concept and who work hard to match the right applicant with the right job and train the applicant thoroughly are normally very successful. Those who fail to put forth the effort are usually rewarded with a failing business.

Because turnover rates in the industry are high and employees seem to come and go, it is far too easy for the supervisor or the manager to start believing that training new employees is not worth the effort. This kind of thinking is a certain recipe for disaster. Professional hospitality industry managers and supervisors are obligated to train their workers, help them become productive, and make them key ambassadors of the establishment. This process will cut down on expensive turnover, hiring the right person for the right job initially is probably the most effective step managers can take when it comes to creating a motivated, dynamic workplace.

9

Employee Relations and Labour Relations

Managers, Supervisors, and Work Leaders

To function well, an organisation needs designated managers and supervisors who have specific enduring assignments. Usually the charge given to such a manager or supervisor is responsibility for continuing operations. In some cases work leaders or forepersons assure that day-to-day operational tasks are completed accurately and on time. The rights and responsibilities of managers, supervisors, and work leaders are different.

Organise work to recognise the real and legal differences between managers, supervisors, and work leaders to:

- Preserve organisational integrity
- Treat each type of employee as anticipated by the Higher Education Employer-Employee Relations Act (HEERA)
- Assure that everyone's rights and responsibilities are respected

HEERA

Under the HEERA most employees including work

leaders can be exclusively represented by an employee organisation. Exclusively represented employees are covered by a labour contract. On their Personnel Action Forms, these rank and file employees have an "E" Employee Relations Code. The Employee Relations Code is assigned to each position by the Human Resources Classification Unit based on a review of the job description or the job vacancy listing. The supervisory exclusion of HEERA is very close to the National Labour Relations Act (NLRA). Case law under NLRA has not generally supported a management structure that establishes supervisors with responsibility for fewer than 2 FTE.

Although supervisors may join and participate in employee organisations, they cannot be exclusively represented on supervisory employer-employee relations issues. Neither can they participate in the same local union as exclusively represented employees. Supervisors have a "C" Employee Relations Code. Managerial employees (Employee Relations Code "A") are not covered by the HEERA and thus have no legal rights to join or participate in employee organisations. A managerial employee is one who has significant responsibilities for formulating or administering policy or programmes.

In addition to managers, confidential employees (Employee Relations Code "F") are also excluded from HEERA and thus have no employee organisational rights. A confidential employee is one who is required to develop or present management's position with respect to negotiations with unions, or whose duties normally require access to confidential information that contributes significantly to the development of such management positions. As a practical matter almost all confidential employees are in Human Resources and the Chancellor's Office.

Tasks of a supervisor

A supervisor must perform at least three of the following tasks to be considered a supervisor under the HEERA:

— Independently selects subordinates OR participates in the interview process and recommends who should be hired to a higher level manager, who customarily gives substantial weight to the recommendation.

— Independently determines the performance ratings and independently communicates them to a subordinate OR the supervisor; initially decides the ratings to be given a subordinate; submits them for review to a higher-level manager who customarily approves the recommended evaluation; and formally communicates the performance evaluation to the subordinate.

— Exercises independent judgment in determining what work is to be done and who will do it OR is given work by a higher-level administrator and then exercises independent judgment to determine the distribution of the work to subordinates.

— Independently decides within budgetary limitations the amount of subordinate merit increases, determines who will be selected for promotional opportunity and decides which positions to recommend for reclassification OR makes recommendations on these actions to a higher level manager, who customarily gives substantial weight to the recommendation.

— Has independent authority to issue written warnings and suspensions OR independently determines what discipline (including dismissal) should be imposed on a subordinate and submits and/or recommends the same for review and/or approval to a higher-level manager, who customarily gives substantial weight to the supervisor's recommendation.

— Has independent authority to resolve grievances or complaints OR independently formulates a resolution to a grievance or complaint and submits the proposed resolution to a higher-level manager, who customarily approves the proposed resolution.

Tasks of a work leader

Usually work leaders spend a substantial portion of their time performing work identical to that assigned to their subordinates who are exclusively represented employees. A work leader typically:

— Distributes work to subordinates according to directions from a higher-level supervisor or follows past practice in distributing work.

— Keeps time records and approves short absences for subordinates.

— Screens applications to verify that mandatory job requirements are met and may participate in selection committees.

— Gathers information relating to an incident that may result in the discipline of a subordinate and refers it to a higher-level manager for appropriate action.

— Receives recommended performance evaluations from the various people for whom his subordinate works, adds none of his own input, and compiles the information into one official performance evaluation.

Managers and supervisors are responsible for representing management in the work place. Thus, it has traditionally been held that it would be a conflict of interest to assign supervisory duties to exclusively represented employees, such as work leaders. You would, in effect, be asking a bargaining unit employee to represent management before another bargaining unit employee.

Because the supervisor/work leader distinction is universally recognised outside the Hotel, arbitrators and agency investigators will make certain assumptions:

— A work leader cannot give direct orders; therefore, failure to follow such orders is not insubordination.

— Work leaders may not be required to perform true supervisory tasks.

— It is difficult to compel a work leader to testify in an arbitration hearing involving another exclusively-represented employee.

Employee Representation

The campus has both exclusively-represented employees and non-represented employees.

Exclusive Representatives

An organisation which has won the right (by employee vote conducted by the PERB) to represent a certain group of employees with related job classifications is known as an exclusive representative. The Hotel may address only that organisation concerning matters of rights for those employees. These employees are covered by a bi-lateral agreement — a labour contract negotiated between the Hotel and the exclusive representative.

Non-Exclusively Represented Employees

Employees including supervisors who are covered by the Personnel Policies for Staff Members do not have exclusive representatives. The Hotel is obligated to notify individual employees of proposed changes in their wages, hours, terms, and conditions of employment, and to meet and discuss those changes with employees or their representatives, including employee organisations.

Representation of Supervisors

Supervisors also have rights under the HEERA to be represented in grievances and in meetings with management regarding their terms and conditions of employment; however, there are legal restrictions on those rights. Supervisory employees cannot elect an exclusive bargaining agent or negotiate collective bargaining agreements. Further, supervisory employees cannot represent non-supervisory employees, or vice versa, in grievances or in discussions with management over wages, hours, or terms and conditions of employment. Managers and confidential employees do not have rights under the HEERA. They may not be represented in grievance matters investigatory interviews by supervisory or rank and file employees.

Employee Complaint Procedures

In any employment situation, disagreements or differences between employees and supervisors can occur. When they do, it is important that you respond quickly and effectively so that a minor issue does not grow into one which cannot be resolved. If informal efforts to resolve a difference or dispute fail, all staff employees have access to a complaint procedure. These complaint procedures provide a precise structure for formally resolving issues in an orderly fashion. If efforts fail to resolve the disagreement or difference at each step of the procedure, certain issues can be submitted to arbitration, in which a third party makes a decision based on evidence and testimony provided at a formal hearing.

The Guiding principles are

— Respond quickly, fairly, and effectively to complaints so that a minor issue doesn't grow into one which cannot be resolved. Conduct a thorough investigation to make informed decisions during the grievance process.

— Work with the employee and the representative, if any, to resolve the problem.

— See all sides of the issues and be willing to change your decision if warranted by the new information gained during the grievance meeting.

Conducting an Investigation

Your most important role in responding to a complaint is to formulate your position on the employee's verbal or written grievance. To make an informed decision that can be supported by your department and the campus, you must know all the facts—adverse facts as well as favorable ones. Thus, you must objectively investigate the assertions made by the employee.

The following guidelines will help you to conduct a thorough investigation:

— Keep records of all matters investigated.

— Who are witnesses and exactly what did they see and hear?

— What documents are pertinent to the complaint?

— How was the investigation conducted? In discipline cases it is important to record the steps of your investigation, such as when the grievant was interviewed, by whom, and who was present.

— Examine the labour agreement or personnel policy cited by the grievant.

— Is the labour agreement or personnel policy provision relevant? Is it ambiguous? How have you generally interpreted the provision? Have you administered this provision consistently?

— Does the labour agreement or personnel policy address the matter in dispute? If so, is there a past practice covering it? Is the practice fixed and established? Has it been relied on before? How long has the practice existed?

— What evidence supports the employee's interpretation of the labour agreement or personnel policy?

— Determine whether other employees have been treated differently under similar circumstances.

— If other employees have been treated differently, what is the reason? What records are available which demonstrate the facts? What records can be compiled to illustrate these facts?

— Determine whether any personal, departmental, political or other issues are pertinent to the complaint.

— Get and study any records that bear on the complaint, such as attendance records (for all employees) and workload measures.

— Do the records clarify the facts? Are any other records available? What can be produced from the records to clarify the facts? Do the facts as clarified support the grievant or management?

— Determine whether the grievance has any equal opportunity implications.

— Identify the resolution the employee or union is seeking.

— Determine the extent of liability.

— Are there class action suit aspects to the grievance?

Once you have formulated your position based on a thorough investigation, you can address the employee's informal complaint. It is best to resolve issues at this stage before positions become hardened and intractable.

The Grievance Meeting

If you cannot resolve a grievance informally you may receive a written grievance, forwarded to you by Human Resources. When you attend meetings to discuss the complaint with the employee, your role is to supply the factual information that supports the action you took and to listen for new information from the employee that could affect your decision. You should be as forthcoming as possible so that the employee and the representative, if any, will fully understand your position. You should also be willing to change your decision if warranted by new information gained during the meeting.

During the grievance meeting, remember the following:

— Maintain a problem-solving approach. Your objective should be to work with the employee and the representative, if any, to resolve a specific problem.

— Avoid taking the grievance personally. Grievances are filed against management, not against individuals.

— Stick to the subject. Avoid getting sidetracked into issues that do not relate specifically to the problem at hand.

— Allow the representative some latitude. The representative is responsible for assertively and constructively presenting the employee's case to management. Some of the advocate's behavior is motivated by the need to maintain an image with employees as someone who does not cower in the presence of management.

— Maintain self control. Losing control during the meeting may cause you to make rash promises or threats. Be aware of posturing; the representative may be trying to put you in a position to make an incorrect decision.

— Be aware of the political implications of the grievance. Unions have internal pressures and are subject to pressures from their constituents. This is why certain grievances are pursued with vigor beyond the importance of the issues.

You can always ask for time to think over the contents of the meeting and to discuss how it is being conducted with the Labour Relations Specialist.

Grievance Procedures

You may have to process complaints using different procedures, which are described in the specific labour agreement or policy covering the employee who files the complaint.

Grievance Settlements

In many cases, after further investigation of information exchanged during grievance meetings, you and/or the employee may change your assessment of the issues in the complaint. Maybe there were extenuating circumstances that you did not know until the meeting; maybe at the meeting the employee came to understand that other employees were treated in the same manner. Further, either party may decide that pursuing the grievance is not as important as settling the complaint; or you could conclude that it is not worth the time, effort, and expense involved in pursuing the matter.

In such cases, Labour Relations can represent you in seeking a no-fault, non-precedent-setting, written settlement with the employee and, if applicable, the union. The specific terms of the settlement agreement are structured to address the precise issues of the grievance. Typically, for grievances involving discipline or dismissal, in exchange for your reducing the penalty, the employee agrees to drop all complaint proceedings against the department , e.g., you exchange the possibility of your two-day suspension prevailing in a grievance hearing with an uncontested letter of warning, which cannot be grieved.

Arbitration of Employee Complaints

When efforts to resolve an employee's complaint through the grievance procedure fail, the employee and/or union can, in certain instances, appeal the matter to arbitration. At an arbitration hearing, a neutral third party hears testimony and reviews written exhibits presented by the employee/union and the Hotel. The neutral party issues a written decision, which in most instances is final and binding on both parties.

Arbitration Under the Collective Bargaining Agreements

Under the labour agreements, only the union can appeal issues to arbitration. The arbitrator, whose decisions are final and binding, is selected from a permanent preapproved panel. Costs are shared equally by the union and the Hotel. Any grievance can be taken to arbitration, but the Hotel may argue at the hearing that a particular issue is non-arbitrable based on the specific wording of the contract provision being arbitrated.

Preparing for the Arbitration Hearing

After the employee or union appeals the grievance to arbitration, you will be contacted by the Labour Relations Specialist in Human Resources who will represent you at the hearing. The Labour Relations Specialist will work with you to decide on the arbitrators you would prefer to hear the grievance. Using the method specified in the appropriate policy or contract, the Labour Relations Specialist and the employee or union will then select the arbitrator. Based on the schedules of all likely arbitration participants, a date for the hearing will be determined by Human Resources. If a non-Hotel arbitrator is selected, the hearing will normally be held approximately two months after selection of the arbitrator. Hearings involving Hotel hearing officers can normally be scheduled sooner.

At the hearing you will be represented by the Labour Relations Specialist. Also in attendance will be one departmental representative (the department chair, the department's chief staff manager, or you); the grievant; the grievant's representative, if any; the arbitrator; and a court reporter or someone operating a tape recorder. The individual labour contract may provide for attendance by others. If the case involves discipline or dismissal, the Hotel presents its case first and must prove that it acted in accordance with the policy or labour agreement provision cited in the employee's grievance. In most other cases, the employee must proceed first and must prove that the cited policy or contract provision was violated.

After an opening statement, the first party questions the witnesses it calls to support its side. Through these witnesses, documents are also entered into evidence. The second party has a chance to cross-examine the witnesses. After the first party completes its case, the second party makes an opening statement, calls its witnesses, and introduces its evidence.

After all the testimony has been presented, both sides can make verbal closing remarks or agree to submit written briefs. The brief usually contains a summary of each party's case and presents arguments to support its position. Briefs are usually due 30 days after the hearing or, if transcripts are made, 30 days after receipt of the transcripts. The arbitrator usually issues a decision within 30 days after the hearing or after the briefs are received.

Notice

When your department or unit is contemplating changes to the working environment that will affect an employee or group of employees, you must provide information about certain kinds of changes to the exclusive representatives . Of course you will want to begin informing your employees about your plans as early as possible. When a proposal has reached the stage of being reasonably certain (but not cast in stone yet), it is time to send information to the unions involved. Notice is the term used to describe this information process. You'll hear it referred to as both a verb and a noun.

For employees not represented by an exclusive representative you are obligated to provide notice directly to the employees. The Hotel has a policy of providing simultaneous notice to employee organisations that have expressed an interest in representing such employees. One way to find out whether notice is needed is to look up the action you are proposing in the contract.

Notice time frames

The lead time for notice depends on the action you are

considering. One issue would be a major reorganisation that could create new reporting lines for employees, necessitate possible layoffs, create new layoff units, or change layoff units. Layoffs require notice to exclusive representatives , before the formal letter to the employee. The terms of the individual contract will identify the notice requirements.

The obligation to provide advance notice of a proposed change in terms and conditions of employment is derived either from the case law interpreting HEERA for not exclusively-representative employees, or from the provisions of the existing labour contract for employees who are exclusively represented.

For non-exclusively-represented employees who have collective bargaining rights (excluding managers and confidential employees), the case law requires the employer to provide reasonable notice of substantial changes in terms and conditions of employment, with the opportunity for the employee to comment before the change is implemented. A reasonable notice period is generally interpreted to be 30 days, although there may be some flexibility in extenuating circumstances.

Since many employees may access their rights to preference for rehire for up to two months before the effective date of a layoff, the earlier you can provide the notice information, the better.

The notice period to the union is not supposed to overlap the formal written letter of layoff, since the notice period is really a proposal stage. Sometimes a union will agree to a department giving the employee the written letter of layoff during the notice period, but with the understanding that the layoff is technically still within the proposal or notice period.

Needed information

If you are considering major changes such as a reorganisation or a layoff of a number of employees, ask your Employee Relations Specialist early in the process what information on will be needed. Often the ERS will schedule a meeting with other Personnel specialists in Employment, Classification, and Labour Relations to help you get the full picture of what may be involved in your proposal.

Labour Relations needs to know:

— Date of the proposed action
— Detailed reason(s) for the proposed action
— Number of and classifications of affected employees
— Policies or contracts under which affected employees are covered (identify each employee by policy or contract)
— If applicable, current and proposed organisation charts
— If a layoff, and if not in seniority order, information on why order is different
— Name, title, phone number of one contact person in the department

When notice is not necessary

Some actions don't call for notice; two examples are a change of assignment or supervisors within the same classification and department. Employees don't have a right to always perform the same set of duties within their classification, nor do they have a right to the same supervisor forever.

Taking Disciplinary Action

All employees are expected to meet performance

standards and behave appropriately in the workplace. Disciplinary or corrective action is a process of communicating with the employee to improve unacceptable behavior or performance. You may take disciplinary action when other methods such as coaching and performance appraisal have not been successful. In cases of serious misconduct, you may choose to proceed straight to disciplinary action. Reviewing the Seven Tests of Just Cause (see next page) before taking disciplinary action will help you determine whether discipline is the best approach to problem-solving in a particular situation.

In carrying out disciplinary action be sure to:

— Build trust and maintain a professional manner by keeping the disciplinary process confidential between you and the employee

— Make a careful diagnosis of the problem to determine whether disciplinary action is appropriate

— Provide specific examples of performance discrepancies or work rule violations so the employee fully understands what needs correction

— Allow the employee ample opportunity to explain so that you have all the facts

— Make sure discipline is the appropriate tool. Would coaching or performance appraisal be sufficient to get the employee's attention?

— When you take disciplinary action, make sure the punishment fits the crime

— Help the employee improve performance by providing specific recommendations and requirements

— Communicate clearly so the employee understands the consequences if performance or conduct does not improve

Disciplinary Alternatives

When deciding what disciplinary action to take, keep in mind that discipline is supposed to be constructive. Your goal is to guide the employee to correct performance or behavior, not to punish the employee. As a general rule, your action should be just enough to get the employee's attention. However, you may have to take progressively more serious actions if there is no improvement or if repeat occurrences follow. You need not take each of these actions, but you will normally take more than one of them. Your alternatives are:

Oral Warning:

— Set a time and place to ensure privacy.

— Make notes about what you want to say in advance.

— Remember that the employee has a right to choose representation.

— State clearly that you are issuing an oral warning.

— Be specific in describing the unacceptable performance or behavior.

— Remind the employee of the acceptable standards or rules. If they are available in writing, provide them to the employee.

— State the consequences of failure to demonstrate immediate and sustained improvement: Further disciplinary action may be the result.

— Note the oral warning on your calendar.

As a supervisor, it is perfectly natural for you to feel frustrated or angry when an employee repeatedly fails to perform satisfactorily or follow the rules. Keep in mind, however, that most employees come to work wanting to do a good job. Some will require more specific and frequent feedback than others to understand what that means in your work site and in the jobs under your supervision. Frequency of feedback will largely depend on what you observe in the employee's behavior and performance and on the cycles of the work (e.g., tardiness can be corrected immediately, but it may take days or weeks to complete a particular project or task for your review).

Remember that the purpose of disciplinary action is to turn performance around by continuing to identify problems, causes, and solutions. If you can accomplish it in a positive and constructive way, you will send a message that you are out not to punish, but to help the employee become a fully productive member of your work unit.

SEPARATIONS

Employees separate from the campus in a variety of ways. Some separations are voluntary and initiated by the employee, such as resignation or retirement. Others are involuntary and initiated by management, such as layoff or medical separation. The death of an employee or dismissal for cause creates unique challenges. Each type of separation requires specific, different actions by you, though some processes are common to all. Your common sense and good judgment will serve you well in response to the special circumstances that arise with each employee's separation. Whatever the circumstances, every employee leaving the campus, whether voluntarily or involuntarily, should feel that she was treated with respect.

Resignation

Employees who voluntarily separate from employment

are considered to have resigned their employment. Requirements for the amount of notice vary, depending on the personnel programme. When an employee becomes unable to perform essential, assigned duties of a position as a result of a disability or medical condition, the campus is committed to providing services to assist the employee, including efforts at reasonable accommodation. If accommodation efforts are unsuccessful, the employee may be medically separated.

Bibliography

Boella, Michael John. *Principles of Hospitality Law*. London: Cassell, 1999.

Carmouche, Rita. *Behavioural Studies in Hospitality Management*. New York: Chapman & Hall, 1995.

Clark, Mona. *Interpersonal Skills for Hospitality Managers*. London: Chapman Hill, 1995.

Forrest, Lewis C. *Training for the Hospitality Industry*. East Lansing: Educational Institute of the American Hotel and Motel Association, 1996.

Go, Frank M. *Human Resource Management in the Hospitality Industry*. New York: Wiley, 1996.

Jordan, Debra J. *Leadership in Leisure Services: Making a Difference*. State College: Venture Pub., 1996.

Kasavana, Michael L. Managing Front Office Operations. Lansing: Educational Institute of the American Hotel and Motel Association, 1995.

Kavanaugh, Raphael R. *Supervision in the Hospitality Industry*. East Lansing: Educational Institute of the American Hotel & Motel Association, 1995.

Kotschevar, Lendal H. Managing Bar and Beverage Operations. East Lansing: Educational Institute of the American Hotel and Motel Association, 1996.

Kudrle, Albert E. Public Relations for Hospitality Managers: Communicating for Greater Profits. New York: Wiley, 1995.

Lucas, Rosemary E. *Managing Employee Relations in the Hotel and Catering Industry*. London: Cassell, 1995.

Miller, Jack E.; Walker, John R.; Drummond, Karen Eich, *Supervision in the Hospitality Industry: Applied Human Resources*. John Wiley & Sons, Inc., 2006

Neufeldt, S. A., "Use of a Manual to Train Supervisors", *Counselor Education and Supervision,* 1994.

Powers, Thomas F. *Introduction to Management in the Hospitality Industry*. New York: Wiley, 1995.

Scott, K. J., Ingram, K. M., Vitanza, S. A., & Smith, N. G., "Training in Supervision: A Survey of Current Practices", *The Counseling Psychologist,* 2000.

Stephen S. Hall, *Ethics in Hospitality Management: A Book of Readings*. Lansing: Educational Institute of the American Hotel and Motel Association, 1992.

Van Hoof, Hubert B. A *Host of Opportunities: An Introduction to Hospitality Management*. Chicago: Irwin, 1996.

Walker, John R. *Introduction to Hospitality Management*. Upper Saddle River, N.J.: Prentice Hall, 2004.

Woods, Robert H. *Managing Hospitality Human Resources*. East Lansing: Educational Institute of the American Hotel & Motel Association, 1997.

Index

Notes